Grid cells (left block): 1, 2, 3, 4, 5, 6, 7, 8, 9, 10, 11, 12, 13, 14, 15, 16, 17, 18, 19, 20, 21, 22, 23, 24, 25, 26, 27, 28, 29, 30

Grid cells (right block): 31, 32, 33, 34, 35, 36, 37, 38, 39, 40, 41, 42, 43, 44, 45, 46, 47, 48, 49, 50, 51, 52, 53, 54, 55, 56, 57, 58, 59, 60

1. Norman Rockwell 1958
2. Dean Cornwell 1959
3. Harold Von Schmidt 1959
4. Fred Cooper 1960
5. Floyd Davis 1961
6. Edward Wilson 1962
7. Walter Biggs 1963
8. Arthur William Brown 1964
9. Al Parker 1965
10. Al Dorne 1966
11. Robert Fawcett 1967
12. Peter Helck 1968
13. Austin Briggs 1969
14. Rube Goldberg 1970
15. Stevan Dohanos 1971
16. Ray Prohaska 1972
17. Jon Whitcomb 1973
18. Tom Lovell 1974
19. Charles Dana Gibson* 1974
20. N.C. Wyeth* 1974

21. Bernie Fuchs 1975
22. Maxfield Parrish* 1975
23. Howard Pyle* 1975
24. John Falter 1976
25. Winslow Homer* 1976
26. Harvey Dunn* 1976
27. Robert Peak 1977
28. Wallace Morgan* 1977
29. J.C. Leyendecker* 1977
30. Coby Whitmore 1978
31. Norman Price* 1978
32. Frederic Remington* 1978
33. Ben Stahl 1979
34. Edwin Austin Abbey* 1979
35. Lorraine Fox* 1979
36. Saul Tepper 1980
37. Howard Chandler Christy* 1980
38. James Montgomery Flagg* 1980
39. Stan Galli 1981
40. Frederic R. Gruger* 1981
41. John Gannam* 1981
42. John Clymer 1982
43. Henry P. Raleigh* 1982
44. Eric (Carl Erickson)* 1982
45. Mark English 1983
46. Franklin Booth* 1983
47. Noel Sickles* 1983
48. John LaGatta* 1984

49. Neysa Moran McMein* 1984
50. James Williamson* 1984
51. Robert Weaver 1985
52. Arthur Burdett Frost* 1985
53. Charles Marion Russell* 1985
54. Al Hirschfeld 1986
55. Rockwell Kent* 1986
56. Maurice Sendak 1987
57. Haddon Sundblom* 1987
58. Robert T. McCall 1988
59. René Bouché* 1988
60. Pruett Carter* 1988

*Presented posthumously

The Society Of Illustrators Thirtieth Annual
Of American Illustration

ILLUSTRATORS

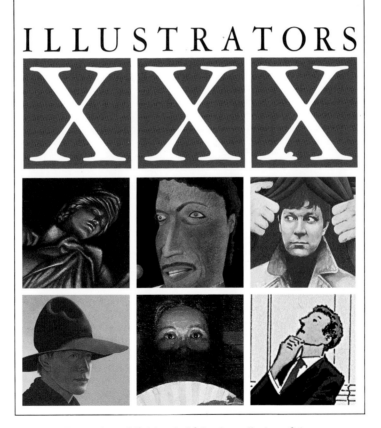

From the exhibition held in the galleries of the
Society of Illustrators Museum of American Illustration
128 East 63rd Street, New York, NY 10021
February 3–April 13, 1988

Society of Illustrators, Inc.
128 East 63rd Street, New York, NY 10021
Copyright © 1989 by Society of Illustrators

ISBN 0-8230-5764-X
Library of Congress Catalog Card Number
59-10849

Distributors to the trade in the United States and
Canada:
Watson-Guptill Publications
1515 Broadway, New York, NY 10036

Distributed throughout the rest of the world by:
Hearst Publications International
105 Madison Avenue, New York, NY 10016

Publisher:
Madison Square Press
10 East 23rd Street, New York, NY 10010

Editor: Art Weithas
Designer: John deCesare
Printed in Japan

The Society Of Illustrators Thirtieth Annual
Of American Illustration

ILLUSTRATORS

XXX

1/30
Published for the Society of Illustrators by Madison Square Press, New York

Portrait: Everett Raymond Kinstler

America's Great Illustrators
by Tom Wolfe

Tom Wolfe, author of *The Right Stuff, The Painted Word,* and the best-selling novel *The Bonfire of the Vanities* and a recognized satirical artist in his own right, graciously gave permission to reprint his review of Susan E. Meyer's *America's Great Illustrators* in this Annual. His commentary on the famous illustrators, both past and present, is as trenchant and perceptive today as when it first appeared in *The New York Times Book Review.* We feel it is an appropriate introduction to this year's celebration of the HALL OF FAME illustrators.

Even the most successful American illustrators of our time who, I would say (since I brought it up), are David Levine, Milton Glaser and Paul Davis—will shed a tear or two over this marvelous book. They were born too late. For all of their talent, I can't see how they or any of their successors can ever compare with J.C. Leyendecker, Charles Dana Gibson, Howard Chandler Christy, James Montgomery Flagg, Frederic Remington or any of the rest of the Great Illustrators of Susan Meyer's title in obtaining what all artists want. What all artists want, Freud assures us, are fame, money and beautiful lovers.

From 1890 to 1920 these rewards were laid upon the top magazine illustrators in job lots. Their celebrity was comparable to that of movie stars after 1920. People used to come down to the railroad station in New Rochelle in the middle of the morning just to watch J.C. Leyendecker and his brother Frank emerge from their limousine and walk to the platform in their matching outfits—e.g., double-breasted blue blazers, white flannels, black-and-white saddle oxfords and ebony-and-white walking sticks—in transit from their 14-room Franco-Suburbo chateau to Studio Leyendecker in New York. Joe Leyendecker lived up, up, up, up, up, to his topmost collar button, to the appearance of his most famous creation, the Arrow Collar Man. The Arrow Collar Man received 17,000 love letters in one month from women who thought he was real.

One of the New Rochelle gawkers, then in his teens, was Norman Rockwell, who resolved to become rich and famous the Leyendecker way. The Leyendecker way

was to do hundreds of covers for The Saturday Evening Post. One of them was the first New Year's Baby with the white satin sash. In those days a few hundred Post covers brought you fame, money, the works—and without the sniggers that Rockwell had to endure when his time came.

Charles Dana Gibson's pen-and-ink drawings of East Coast Society for the old Life featured the Gibson Girl, a romantic archetype with a popular impact equal to that of Valentino, Garbo, Bogart and Gable in the movies later on. Two plays, "The Gibson Play" and the highly successful "Mr. Pipp" (also made into a movie), were based on characters in Gibson drawings; many songs and stage shows used the Gibson Girl as a theme, and innumerable stories, novels and advertising campaigns appropriated her indirectly. In 1903 a bidding war for Gibson's services resulted in a contract from Collier's giving him $100,000 for 100 pen-and-ink drawings. During the First World War Gibson became a patriotic figure, as revered as Sir Philip Sidney in England 350 years before, thanks to his role in mobilizing the leading illustrators for martial propaganda. His

friend James Montgomery Flagg produced his "Uncle Sam Wants You" poster for the glorious Gibson campaign. France made Gibson a chevalier of the Legion of Honor. Belgium made him an officer of the Crown, and the United States poured as much eulogistic oratory over Gibson as over Pershing.

As Susan Meyer points out, however, the Great Ones' flaming High-Rent priapic success was not due simply, or even mainly, to genius, although some of them, notably Gibson, Howard Pyle, N.C. Wyeth and John Held, had genius to burn. The truth was that they had the good fortune to be working in *the* great age of magazine illustration. The period 1880 to 1930 was the half-century in which the magazine industry grew up and boomed, and magazines became the dominant form of popular entertainment. Magazine illustration idealized and reshaped popular taste in a way that film and, to some extent, comic strips would after 1920.

As for Flagg, he was as famous, high-living, grossly gossiped about and generally swell a figure as his pal John Barrymore. Flagg created the Flagg Girl as a more carnal version of the Gibson Girl, and his affairs with his models ran through the newspaper columns like a rogue hormone. Flagg was among the first of many 20th-century celebrities to discover that lubricious notoriety did not hurt a bit. He loved to say things such as: "Many of those girls were so beautiful, and artists are such *fools*! If I had this side of life to live over again, I'd again be just such a a fool as I was."

But Leyendecker, Gibson and their confrères had another great advantage as well. What would later become a severe split in status between illustration and fine art (in the form of easel painting) barely affected these men, with the exception of the last of the line,

Rockwell. So much of the prestigious painting of the 19th century was itself illustration (from David and Delacroix to Mount and Bingham) that the world "illustrator," designating a separate category of artists, did not exist before 1850. As late as 1900 artists moved back and forth from easel painting to commercial illustration without any real sense of crossing a boundary line. Many of the most important innovations of the period of Art Nouveau, such as Beardlsey's and Toulouse Lautrec's, originated in commercial illustration. The German magazine Simplicissimus had Bruno Paul, Olaf Gulbransson, Heinrich Kley, Eduard Thöny, Thomas Theodor Heine, Rudolf Wilke, Kathe Kollwitz and George Grosz all working for it during the same period.

A key fact was that the training of illustrators and easel painters was precisely the same: i.e., both were trained to illustrate. But by the 1950's "fine art" and "graphic art" instruction had come to mean two very different things, even though it was fashionable to insist that no such distinctions existed. No one insisted more fashionably than Bauhaus artists such as Josef Albers. Yet during Albers's reign as dean of the Yale art school, talented young artists from all over the country came to New Haven and got the true message immediately: Illustration was superficial stuff, tolerable only if the artist used an obsolete medium such as the woodcut, the steel engraving, the etching or the lithograph (although the lithograph was dangerously modern). One of Albers's many *obiter dicta* was that the purpose of art is "to present, not to represent." Albers's own reputation as an artist was based on the 30 years he had spent working out the problems (if any) of painting geometric shapes in flat colors. He spent 15 years on squares alone. It was little enough, then, to ask the young artist at Yale to spend his first year sitting at a table placing squares of Color-aid paper one upon the other while Albers peered over his shoulder looking for signs of genius.

Albers's interminable squares became the symbol of the divorce of fine art from rude passion and, for that matter, from direct experience altogether. For example, as Cubism was followed by Abstract Expressionism and Pop Art and Color Field and Hard Edge and Minimal and Conceptual Art, sexuality vanished to a quite extraordinary degree. It showed up only in such sport forms as Tom Wesselmann's Doublemint Airbrush-style aureolae and the occasional hard-rutting Eurosodomites in the work of Francis Bacon. Even Pop Art drew not upon real life—the theory was explicit on the point—but upon commercial art, in a camp approximation of the way Picasso and Braque drew upon primitive art.

Given the sway that such theories have held in the universities, not to mention the galleries and museums, the wonder is that illustrators the caliber of David Levine, Milton Glaser and Paul Davis emerge at all today. Illustrators have to go back 50 years or more if they want to find usable models among eminent painters. Mr. Levine's sources are 19th-century artists such as Cruikshank and André

Gill, and antecedents of Mr. Glaser's highly original style are in Art Nouveau. Others, particularly fantasists such as Frank Frazetta, go straight back to the first man in Susan Meyer's gallery, Howard Pyle.

Humbled though they may be by its Golden Aztec vision of illustration's lost past, illustrators will study this book religiously. It is one of the few art books I know of that will engage artists on a professional, technical level, and at the same time delight them and readers generally with its splendid picture plates and its Lives of the Artists. The text gives detailed descriptions of how these illustrators worked. We see Maxfield Parrish spending hours using glazes to achieve his luminous Lafayette blues and tawny apricots. We also see his (and Norman Rockwell's) rather less glorious use of photographic projections, resulting in insipid human forms.

Susan Meyer avoids the curse of practically all art books: the temptation to play god or sycophant or worshiper and assign each artist to a cloud in Art Heaven. She does not inflate the abilities of these men and she does not condescend to them. She analyzes them. She offers the best analysis of the complex designs of John Held's famous flapper drawings that I have ever read, and she publishes 13 of his paintings for the first time (that I know of). One of them, called "Cows Watching Plane," is by itself, for my money, worth the heavy price of this book. □

The great illustrators mentioned by Tom Wolfe in his review are all members of the Society of Illustrators Hall of Fame with one exception: John Held, Jr. who humorously encapsulated the Roaring Twenties. He may be just patiently waiting in the wings.

The Thirtieth Anniversary of
the Hall of Fame

Beginning with Howard Pyle, the grandfather of American Illustration and including such greats as Frederic Remington, N.C. Wyeth, J.C. Leyendecker, Charles Dana Gibson and Norman Rockwell, the Society of Illustrators presents a selection of illustrators (1880-1940) elected to the Hall of Fame since its conception in 1958. These artists, plus their contemporaries,* project a glowing panorama of an ever-changing America for more than a century.

Howard Pyle: 1853-1911
The Battle of Bunker Hill
Collection of the Delaware Art Museum, Wilmington

*The Hall of Fame contemporary illustrators appear in the Museum Exhibitions section entitled Hall of Fame (1940-1988).

Frederic Sackrider Remington 1861-1909
"The Old Stage Coach of the Plains"

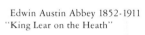

A.B. Frost 1851-1928
"The Conciliator"

Maxfield Parrish 1870-1966
"Pierrot's Serenade"

Charles Dana Gibson 1867-1944
"At the Recital"

Edwin Austin Abbey 1852-1911
"King Lear on the Heath"

"Doctor and Ballerina"

Robert T. McCall (b. 1919)

Hall of Fame 1988

A merica's best known space artist, Robert McCall, lives and works in Paradise Valley, Arizona, on a street appropriately named Moonlight Way. McCall was born in 1919 in Columbus, Ohio, to parents who encouraged his early interest in art. He won a scholarship to Columbus School of Fine Art and by age 17 was working as a part-time commercial artist.

During World War II, McCall served with the Army Air Corps, sketching airplanes whenever possible. In 1945 he met and married Louise Harrup, an art student, who has collaborated with him over a 43 year period. Today they have two daughters and five grandchildren.

In 1949 the McCalls moved to New York where Bob began illustrating for *The Saturday Evening Post, Collier's,* and various advertising agencies. Among his many commissions for *Life* magazine was a series of paintings on the future of space flight. When the National Aeronautics and Space Administration initiated a Fine Art Program, McCall was assigned to cover the Mercury, Gemini, and Apollo missions.

McCall designed and painted the massive six-story-high mural depicting man's conquest of the Moon for the National Air and Space Museum in Washington, D.C., produced another mural for the Johnson Space Center in Texas, and one at the Dryden Flight Research Facility in California. In addition to these monumental

works, McCall has designed stamps for the U.S. Postal Service commemorating the historic missions into space. His "Decade of Achievement" stamp was cancelled on the Moon before a world-wide television audience.

Not only is McCall a documenter of actual events, he is a visionary of man's future in space. He created conceptual paintings for "2001: A Space Odyssey," and art for the films "Meteor," 'Star Trek," and Disney's space thriller, "The Black Hole."

In 1977, McCall covered the Approach and Landing Tests of the Space Shuttle Enterprise, and four years later joined a NASA art team to cover the first launch of the Space Shuttle Columbia. He was assigned to suit-up activity as astronauts John Young and Bob Crippen prepared for their first Space Shuttle flight.

McCall has said, "I can't be one of the astronauts going into space, but at least I can be there to watch their launches and landings. With this kind of close association I am better able to make my paintings more convincing—more believable." ☐

Robert Schulman
Director, NASA Art Program

"First Men to Mars" NASA

James McMullan

Hamilton King Award 1988

The Hamilton King Award is presented annually for the finest illustration in the Annual Exhibition by a member of the Society of Illustrators. The selection is made by the former recipients of this award. The 1988 winner is James McMullan for his poster illustration for the play "Death and the King's Horseman" which appeared at the Lincoln Center Theatre.

Terry Brown: The Hamilton King Award is special. Congratulations!

James McMullan: Thanks. I'm proud to receive it.

TB: The play, "Death and the King's Horseman"—what was it about?

JM: It's a play about ritual suicide, with undertones of reaching for a good and noble death.

TB: Did you watch rehearsals?

JM: Yes, they helped give me the feeling of the dance and of the formalized oratory. I knew that the play would probably have a special, artistic audience who would see that even though the subject matter is dark and somber, it is, nevertheless, a vigorous story. I tried to capture that energy. Jim Russek is one of those rare art directors who gives illustrators space to operate, knowing they will do their best work given only subject and size.

TB: What has been the progression of your life?

JM: I was born in Tsingtao in Northern China where my grandfather was an Anglican minister and my father had a trading agency. When the war came, we were all lucky to reach the last repatriation boat out of Shanghai.

TB: What art schools did you attend besides those in China and Canada?

JM: The Cornish Art School in Seattle and Pratt Institute in New York.

TB: Was it a smooth transition after that?

JM: Yes, I concentrated on book jackets and got some magazine work ... *Seventeen, Esquire,* and *Sports Illustrated.*

TB: Your illustration for the *New York* magazine article, "Tribal Rites of the New Saturday Night," is credited with being the seed for the movie "Saturday Night Fever." Is that true?

JM: It's true. Robert Stigwood said he would never have read the story if my artwork had not caught his attention, and Clay Felker, the publisher, felt that the illustrations, which were completed first, affected the writing.

TB: What was the "invention" in "Death and the King's Horseman"?

JM: I worked a long time on the man's stance, so I suppose that is the basic invention, but I was also happily surprised by what happened when I decided to work back into the dark washes with an opaque blue line.

TB: Do you still teach at the School of Visual Arts?

JM: Yes, I teach drawing and enjoy working with students at an early age, before they've had too many influences.

TB: Do awards such as the Hamilton King Award help?

JM: Yes. Illustration is such solitary work. If you're ambitious and take risks, it's satisfying to have some validation. Awards seem to suggest that somebody out there is looking. □

"Death and the King's Horseman" for Lincoln Center

President's Message

This thirtieth edition of *The Society of Illustrators Annual of American Illustration* represents an exhibition of works from across the nation, revealing the full spectrum of vision and genius in our profession. Although we may debate whether one show is better than the next or which illustration should be recognized as "best," it is impossible to view these exhibitions without feeling impressed and inspired.

The art of illustration mirrors and influences our culture. The exhibitions present standards of excellence. These Annuals, spanning three decades, have become a visual history of American illustration.

This year we celebrate the thirtieth anniversary of the Hall of Fame, a rich heritage of artists who have illuminated our lives. A tribute to the excellence of our profession!

I wish to express gratitude to the many people involved in producing this handsome publication and annual exhibition. We are enriched because of their dedication.

Diane Dillon
President

Portrait: Kinuko Y. Craft

Chairman's Message

My words of congratulations to all those selected for this 30th Illustrators Annual will soon be forgotten, but these works will endure forever. This Annual is a showcase of the entire field of contemporary illustration. It is high praise, indeed, to have one's work selected by one's fellow illustrators.

A word of thanks should be given to all those who contributed to this Annual whether or not their work appears in it. There were far more entries than those selected to be published. I'd like to thank the jurors who gave up their time to judge the 8,000 plus entries that were submitted for this 30th Annual. Also, a special thank you should go to the publisher for organizing this tremendous volume into such a beautiful format.

CHRIS SPOLLEN

Chris Spollen
Chairman, Illustrators 30

Portrait: Jim Sharpe

ANNUAL SHOW
CHAIRMEN

'59 David K. Stone
'60 Harry Carter
'61 Len Jossel
'62 Al Muenchen
'63 George Samerjan
'64 Don Moss
'65 Jerry McDaniel
'66 Gerald McConnell
'67 Shannon Stirnweis
10 Harry Schaare
11 Chuck McVicker
12 Alvin Pimsler
13 Marbury Brown
14 Al Pisano
15 James Crowell
16 Bob Cuevas

17 Roland Descombes
18 Warren Rogers
19 Howard Koslow
20 Doug Johnson
21 Eileen Hedy Schultz
22 Sandy Huffaker
23 Bernie Karlin
26 Roland Descombes
27 Barney Plotkin
28 John Witt
29 Jim Sharpe

Award Winners

Editorial

GOLD MEDAL

Guy Billout

GOLD MEDAL

Blair Drawson

GOLD MEDAL

Richard Mantel

SILVER MEDAL

Julian Allen

SILVER MEDAL

John Craig

SILVER MEDAL

Elwood H. Smith

Jury

GERRY GERSTEN
Chairman
Caricaturist and
Illustrator

WALTER BERNARD
Graphic Designer,
WBMG, Inc.

LOU BROOKS
Illustrator and Designer

PAUL DAVIS
Graphic Designer
and Illustrator

JOHN deCESARE
deCesare Design
Associates

BILL NELSON
Illustrator

REX PETEET
Partner,
Sibley Peteet Design

BURT SILVERMAN
Illustrator

WALT SPITZMILLER
Illustrator

GUY BILLOUT

A native of France, Guy Billout was born in Decise in 1941. He studied advertising at Ecole des Arts Appliques de Beaune in Burgundy, then worked as a designer in advertising agencies in Paris.

In 1969 Billout moved to New York and began illustrating for most of the major magazines, and since 1982 has had a regular feature in *The Atlantic Monthly.* He has also written and illustrated five children's books, four of which were chosen by *The New York Times* for their list of ten best in that category.

1   **GUY BILLOUT**
Art Director: Judy Garlan
Magazine: Atlantic Monthly
Award: Gold Medal

BLAIR DRAWSON

Trained as a painter, Blair Drawson to this day considers himself "a painter who illustrates." He wishes that distinctions which apparently separate illustration from fine art would disappear forever. He lives in Canada with his wife and two children.

2   **BLAIR DRAWSON**
Art Directors: Tom Staebler /
              Bruce Hansen
Magazine: Playboy
Award: Gold Medal

RICHARD MANTEL

A Pratt Institute graduate, Mantel has worked as an illustrator, art director, designer, and currently operates his own Illustration/Design Studio.

He was Art Director of Columbia Records, Atlantic Records, CTI Records, and was a member of Push Pin Studio from 1977 to 1981.

He received awards from the Art Directors Club, Society of Illustrators, *Graphis*, AIGA, *CA, American Illustration,* Society of Publication Designers, and a Grammy for Best Record Jacket.

3   **RICHARD MANTEL**
Art Director: Fred Woodward
Magazine: Texas Monthly
Award: Gold Medal

JULIAN ALLEN

Born in Cambridge, England, Julian Allen studied at the Cambridge College of Art and the Central College of Art and Design in London. After six years as a fashion illustrator, he turned to journalistic illustration and worked primarily for the *London Times Magazine.*

In 1973 he moved to the U.S. to work for *New York* magazine. He has since worked for most American and European magazines and teaches at Parsons School of Design.

4
JULIAN ALLEN
Art Director: Fred Woodward
Magazine: Regardie's
Award: Silver Medal

JOHN CRAIG

Collector, countryman, collage artist, John Craig has built a life and career out of his interst in old postcards and labels.

His first job was as an apprentice to one of the last wood engraving companies. The skills he acquired there he has since incorporated into his collage art.

A native of Pittsburgh, he studied art at Rochester Institute of Technology and the Art Institute of Chicago. He currently lives in Wisconsin.

5   **JOHN CRAIG**
Art Directors: Kerig Pope /
            Karen Gutowsky
Magazine: Playboy
Award: Silver Medal

ELWOOD H. SMITH

Born in Alpena, Michigan in 1941, Elwood Smith attended art school in Chicago, then moved to New York City in 1976. There he rediscovered George Herriman and Company and made a connection to his own past and own voice.

In 1982 he moved out of the city, married, got some dogs and cats and became a "stepappy," as he calls it.

His humorous illustrations have appeared in such publications as the *Chicago Tribune, Fortune* and *Humor.*

6   **ELWOOD H. SMITH**
Art Directors: Kerry Tremain /
                   Hans Teensma
Client: Medical Selfcare
Award: Silver Medal

▲ 7   **ROBERT M. CUNNINGHAM**
Art Director: Debora E. Clark
Magazine: Money Maker

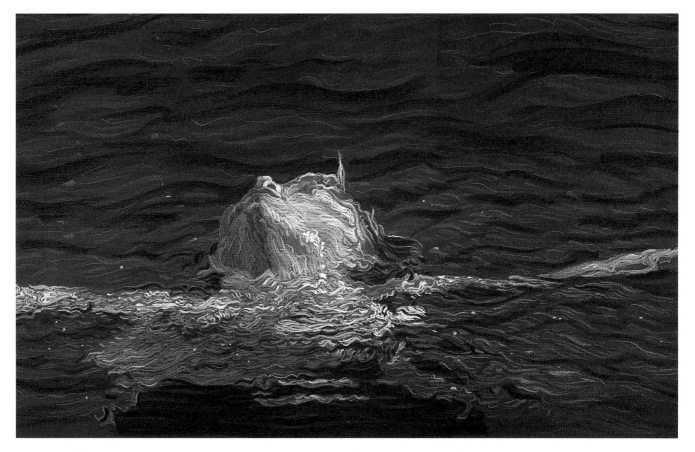

▲ 8 **BILL JAMES**

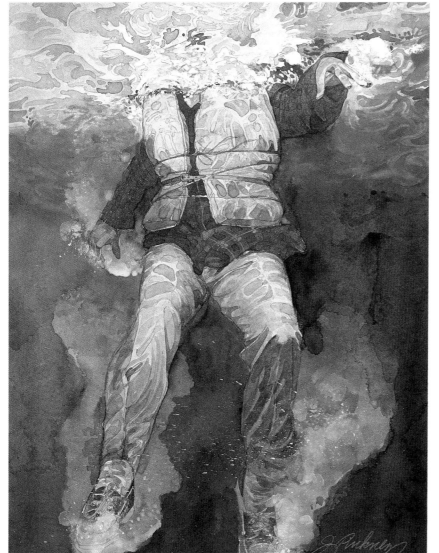

◀ 9 **JERRY PINKNEY**
Art Director: Roger Dowd
Client: Medical Economics

▲ 10   **KEN MARSCHALL**
Art Director: Gerard A. Valerio
Magazine: National Geographic

▲ 11   **KEN MARSCHALL**
Art Director: Gerard A. Valerio
Magazine: National Geographic

▲ 12 **CHARLES REID**
Art Director: Beth Whitaker
Magazine: American Heritage

▶ 13 **HATLEY NORTON MASON III**
Art Director: Howard Shintaku
Client: Sacramento Bee Newspaper

▲ 14   **PHILIP CASTLE**
Art Directors: Rudy Hoglund / Nigel Holmes
Magazine: Time

▲ 18   **JACK UNRUH**
Art Director: Joe Connolly
Magazine: Boy's Life

▲ 19   **ROBERT GIUSTI**
Art Director: Tom Staebler
Magazine: Playboy

▲ 20   **BRIAN AJHAR**
Art Director: Karen Anderson
Magazine: U.S. Air

◀ 21   **ETIENNE DELESSERT**
Art Director: Veronique Vienne
Client: Parenting

◀ 22   **MICHAEL PARASKEVAS**
Art Director: Jane Palecek
Magazine: Hippocrates

▲ 23 **FRED OTNES**
Art Director: Judy Garlan
Magazine: Atlantic Monthly

▶ 24 **FRED OTNES**
Art Director: Judy Garlan
Magazine: Atlantic Monthly

◀ 25   **DAVID WILCOX**
Art Directors: Tom Staebler /
              Kerig Pope
Magazine: Playboy

▼ 26   **KIRA YOKOYAMA**
Art Director: Danielle Gallo
Magazine: Penthouse Letters

▲ 27   **BRAD HOLLAND**
Art Director: Hans-Georg Pospischil
Magazine: Frankfurter Allgemeine

◀ 28   **JEFF MEYER**
Art Director: Victoria Vaccarello
Magazine: Milwaukee

▲ 29   **BRAD HOLLAND**
Art Director: Brian Noyes
Magazine: Washington Post

▲ 30   **TOM CURRY**
Art Director: Judy Garlan
Magazine: Atlantic Monthly

▲ 31   **ALAN REINGOLD**
Art Director: Richard Bleiweiss
Magazine: Penthouse

◄ 32   **TOM CURRY**
Art Director: Judy Garlan
Magazine: Atlantic Monthly

▲ 33   **JIM SHARPE**
Client: ABC "Our World 1972"

▼ 35   **WILLIAM V. CIGLIANO**
Art Directors: Judie Anderson / Dan Jursa
Magazine: Chicago Tribune

▲ 34   **ALAN REINGOLD**
Art Director: D. J. Stout
Magazine: Texas Monthly

▲ 36   **WILLIAM LOW**
Art Director: Rosslyn A. Frick
Client: Amiga World

▲ 37   **C. F. PAYNE**
Art Director: David Harris
Magazine: D

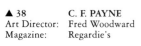

▲ 38   **C. F. PAYNE**
Art Director: Fred Woodward
Magazine: Regardie's

▲ 39   **C. F. PAYNE**
Art Director: D. J. Stout
Client: Texas Monthly

▲ 40 **BLAIR DRAWSON**
Art Directors: Tom Staebler / Kerig Pope
Magazine: Playboy

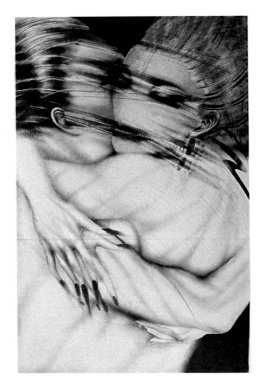

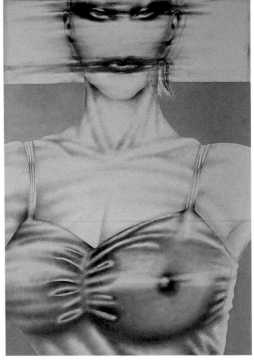

▲ 41 **MARZENA KAWALEROWICZ**
Art Director: Danielle Gallo
Magazine: Penthouse Letters

▲ 42 **MARZENA KAWALEROWICZ**
Art Director: Danielle Gallo
Magazine: Penthouse Letters

▲ 43   **TERRY WIDENER**
Art Directors: Karen Gutowsky / Tom Staebler
Magazine: Playboy

▲ 44   **TERRY WIDENER**
Art Directors: Steven Hoffman / Edward Truscio
Magazine: Sports Illustrated

▲ 45   **JEFF SEAVER**
Art Director: Gary Gretter
Magazine: Sports Afield

▶ 46   **GARY KELLEY**
Art Director: D. J. Stout
Magazine: Texas Monthly

▲ 47   **COBY WHITMORE**
Art Director: Mary Carroll
Magazine: Heritage Classic MCI

◄ 48   **BOB NEWMAN**
Art Director: Miriam Smith
Magazine: Newsday

◀ 49   MALCOLM T. LIEPKE

▲ 50 **JOHN JINKS**
Art Director: Wendy Reingold
Magazine: World Tennis

◀ 51 **GWYN STRAMLER**
Art Director: Tina Adamek
Magazine: Postgraduate Medicine

▲ 52   **VIVIENNE FLESHER**
Art Director: Gail Anderson
Magazine: Boston Globe

▲ 53   **JOHN CLEMENTSON**
Art Director: Neal Pheifer
Magazine: GQ

▲ 54   **SHERILYN VANVALKENBURGH**
Art Director: Lois Erlacher
Magazine: Emergency Medicine

◀ 55   **GERRY GERSTEN**
Art Directors: Nick Meglin /
               Lenny Brenner
Magazine: Mad

▶ 57 **JOHN KASCHT**
Art Director: Jane Palecek
Client: Washington Times

▲ 56 **GERRY GERSTEN**
Art Directors: Nick Meglin /
Lenny Brenner
Magazine: Mad

◀ 58 **STEVE BRODNER**
Art Director: Michael Walsh
Magazine: Washington Post

▲ 59   **STEVE BRODNER**
Art Director: Michael Walsh
Magazine: Washington Post

▲ 60   **BARRY G. PITTS**
Art Director: David Henry
Client: George Paige and Associates

◀ 61   **SUZY PARKER**
Art Director: Richard Curtis
Magazine: USA Today

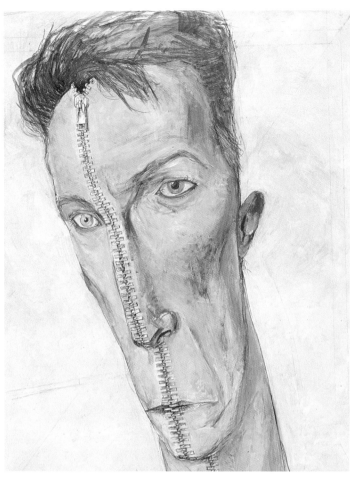

◀ 62   **DANIEL SWEETMAN**
Art Director: Gary Koepke
Magazine: Musician

▼ 63   **KINUKO Y. CRAFT**
Art Directors: Tom Staebler / Kerig Pope
Magazine: Playboy

▲ 64   **BURT SILVERMAN**
Art Directors: Rudy Hoglund / Irene Ramp
Magazine: Time

▲ 65   **BURT SILVERMAN**
Art Director: Cynthia Davis
Magazine: Bicycle Guide

▲ 66   **BURT SILVERMAN**
Art Directors: Kit Lukas / Jane Schulberg
Client: P.B.S.

▶ 67   **TERESA FASOLINO**
Art Director: Jessica Weber
Magazine: Book of the Month Club News

▲ 68   **SEYMOUR CHWAST**
Art Directors: Eloise Vega / George Pierson
Client: HBO

▲ 69　　ELWOOD H. SMITH
Art Director:　Karen Anderson
Magazine:　US Air

▲ 70　　ELWOOD H. SMITH
Art Director:　Michael Walsh
Magazine:　Washington Post

▲ 71   SCOTT SNOW
Art Director: Scott Snow
Client: KSL-TV News

◀ 72   SERGIO CUAN

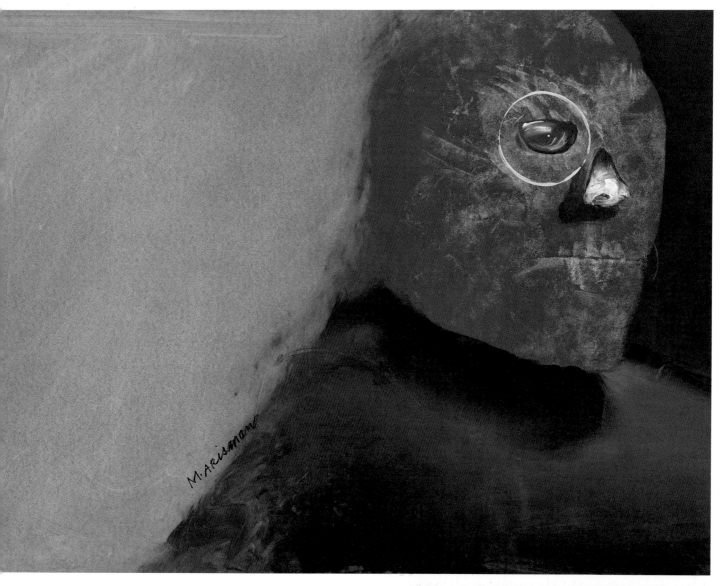

▲ 73   MARSHALL ARISMAN
Art Director: Rip Georges
Magazine: Regardie's

▶ 74   DAN KIRK
Art Director: Malcolm Frouman
Magazine: Business Week

▲ 75   **MARIA RUOTOLO**

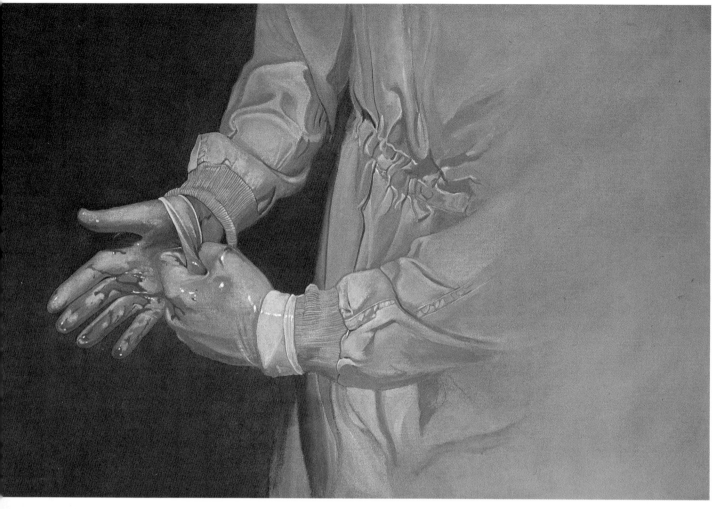

▲ 76 **STEVEN STROUD**
Art Director: Lois Erlacher
Magazine: Emergency Medicine

▶ 77 **HARVEY DINNERSTEIN**
Art Director: Diana LaGuardia
Magazine: New York Times

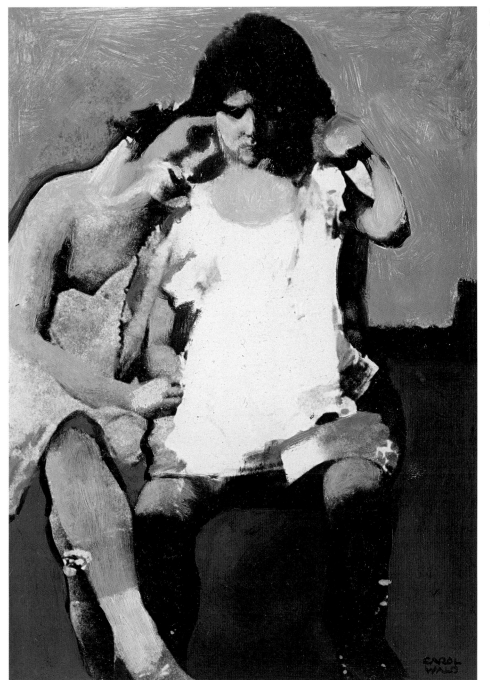

◀ 78   CAROL WALD
Art Director: Tina Klem

▲ 79   CAROL WALD

◀ 80   CAROL WALD
Art Director: Lois Erlacher

CAPTAIN CHARLES NUNGESSER

▲ 81   **ALAN E. COBER**
Art Director: Lee Battaglia
Client: Smithsonian Institution

▲ 82   **ALAN E. COBER**
Art Director: Fred Woodward
Magazine: Texas Monthly

▲ 83   **DANIEL ZAKROCZEMSKI**
Art Director: Joseph Yacinski
Magazine: Changing Times

◀ 84   **LINDA SCHARF**
Art Director: Mary Cristoph
Magazine: Magazine Design and Production

▲ 85   **DOUG GRISWOLD**
Art Director: Brad Zucroff
Client: San Jose Mercury News

◀ 86   **LINDA SCHARF**
Art Director: Marilu Lopez
Magazine: Ms.

▶ 87 **JOHN CRAIG**
Art Director: Kent Barton
Magazine: Sunshine

▼ 88 **JOHN CRAIG**
Art Directors: Roger Gorman /
Malcolm Frouman
Magazine: Business Week

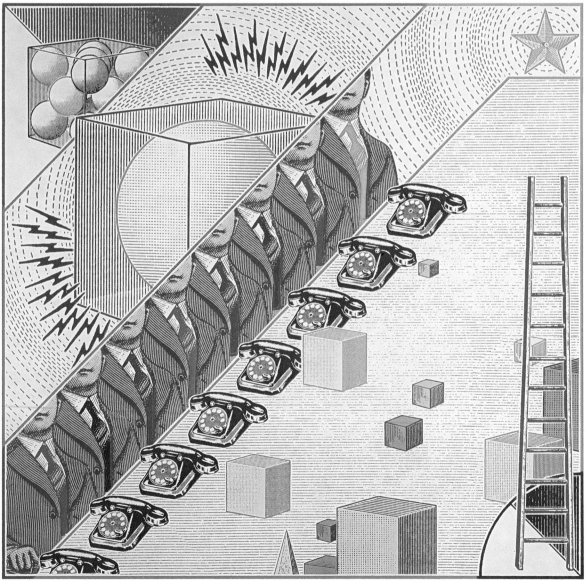

▲ 89   **JAMES MCMULLAN**
Art Director: John Bark
Client: Esquire Magazine

◄ 90   **JAMES MCMULLAN**
Art Director: Norman Hotz
Client: Reader's Digest

▲ 91   **EDWARD SOREL**
Art Director: Everett Halvorsen
Magazine: Forbes

▲ 92   **EVERETT PECK**
Art Director: Michael Rey
Magazine: California

▲ 93   **KAREN BARBOUR**
Art Director: Michele Y. Washington
Magazine: Essence

▲ 94 **WILSON MCLEAN**
Art Director: Kerig Pope
Client: Playboy Magazine

▶ 95 **WILSON MCLEAN**
Art Director: Rudy Hoglund
Client: Time Magazine

▲ 96 **WILLIAM CONE**
Art Director: Rudy Vanderlans
Magazine: Emigre

◀ 97 **WILLIAM CONE**
Art Director: Veronique Vienne
Magazine: Media Alliance

▲ 98   **GUY BILLOUT**
Art Director: Judy Garlan
Magazine: Atlantic Monthly

▲ 99 **GUY BILLOUT**
Art Directors: Tom Staebler /
Theo Kouvatsos
Magazine: Playboy

◀ 100 **GUY BILLOUT**
Art Director: Judy Garlan
Magazine: Atlantic Monthly

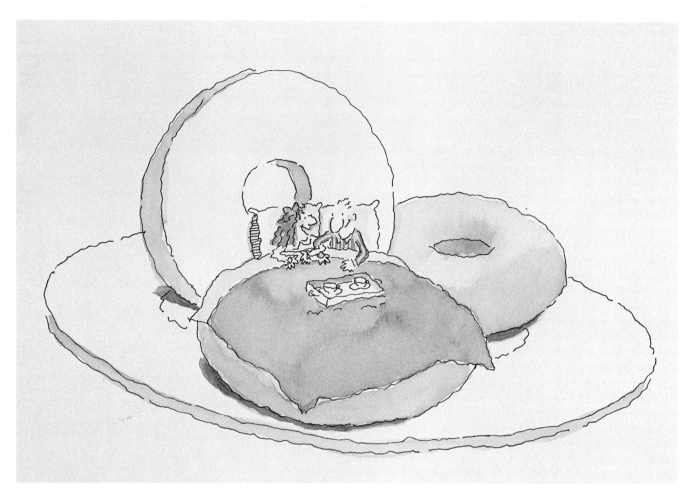

▲ 101   **SUSAN SMITH**
Art Director: Alan Shapiro
Client: Epicurean Express

▲ 102   **GARY VISKUPIC**
Art Director: Bob Eisner
Magazine: Newsday

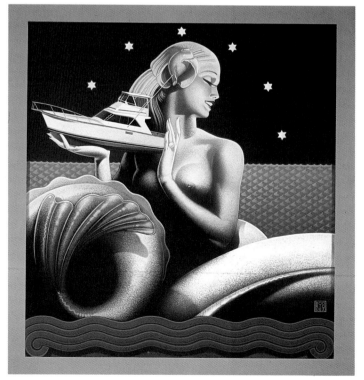

▲ 103   **ROBERT RODRIGUEZ**
Art Director: Marcia Lerner
Magazine: Power & Motoryacht

▲ 104   **TOM SCIACCA**
Art Director: Richard Mantel
Magazine: New York

▲ 105   **LANE SMITH**
Art Director: Sue Llewellyn
Magazine: Stereo Review

▲ 106 **BARBARA NESSIM**
Art Director: Suzanne Zumpano
Client: Simon & Schuster

▲ 107 **BARBARA NESSIM**
Art Directors: Anna Demchick / Mary Shanahan
Magazine: G.Q.

▲ 108 **ANTHONY RUSSO**
Art Director: Rip Georges
Magazine: Regardie's

▶ 109 **ANTHONY RUSSO**
Art Director: Lucy Bartholomay
Magazine: Boston Globe

▶ 110 **ANTHONY RUSSO**
Art Director: Rip Georges
Magazine: Regardie's

▲ 111   AMY GUIP

▲ 112   **ROB DAY**
Art Director: Kurt Conner
Magazine: Indianapolis

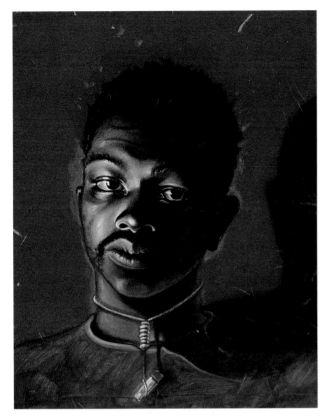

▲ 113   **EARL KELENY**
Art Director: Santa Choplin
Magazine: Florida

▲ 114   **CARY HENRIE**
Art Director: Tina Adamek
Magazine: Postgraduate Medicine

▲ 115   **JOHN HOWARD**
Art Director: Sue Llewellyn
Magazine: Stereo Review

JUDY FILIPPO
Art Director: Douglas Parker
Magazine: Bostonia

▲ 118   **TIM LEWIS**
Art Director: Jennifer Napoli
Magazine: Insurance Review

◀ 117   **TIM LEWIS**
Art Director: Joseph Doyle
Magazine: Business Week Careers

◀ 119   **DAVE CUTLER**
Art Director: Forbes Linkhorn
Magazine: American Journal of Nursing

▲ 120   **TIM BORGERT**
Art Director: Ted Pitts
Client: Dayton Daily News

◀ 121   **STEVE JOHNSON**
Art Director: Chris Greco
Magazine: Mpls. St. Paul

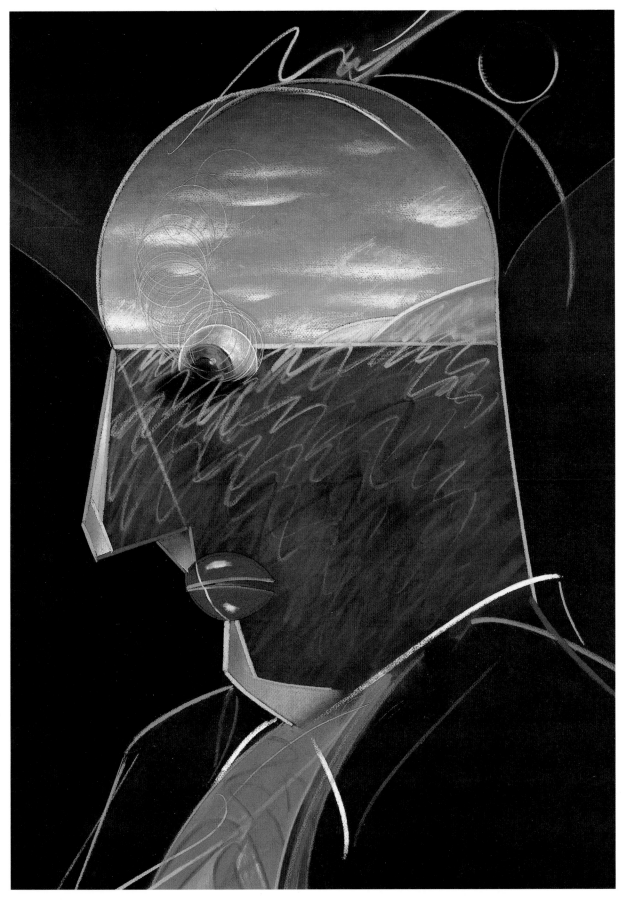

▲ 122   **ANDRZEJ DUDZINSKI**
Art Director: Jane Palecek
Magazine: Hippocrates

▲ 123   **TIM JONKE**
Art Director: David Mocarski

▲ 124   **STEVE BRENNAN**

▲ 125   **ALAN MAGEE**
Art Director: Judy Garlan
Magazine: Atlantic Monthly

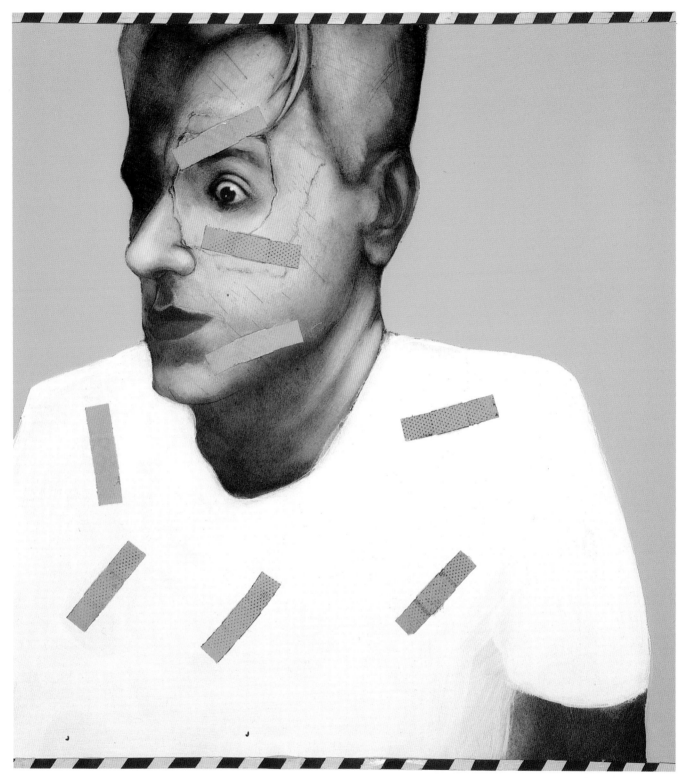

▲ 126   **JOEL PETER JOHNSON**
Art Director: John Davis
Magazine: Buffalo

▲ 128   **JULIAN ALLEN**
Art Director: Veronique Vienne
Magazine: Parenting Magazine

▲ 129   **G. ALLEN GARNS**
Art Director: Gail Anderson
Magazine: Boston Globe

◄ 127   **JOANIE SCHWARZ**
Art Director: Ann Weber
Magazine: Medical Economics

Award Winners

Book

GOLD MEDAL

Paul Davis

SILVER MEDAL

Robert Goldstrom

SILVER MEDAL

John H. Howard

SILVER MEDAL

John H. Howard

Jury

HODGES SOILEAU
Chairman
Illustrator

DOUG JOHNSON
Illustrator

GARY KELLEY
Illustrator

LOUISE KOLLENBAUM
Design Director
of Banana Republic
Travel Clothing Co.

FRED OTNES
Illustrator

MARGERY PETERS
Art Director,
Fortune Magazine

GREG SPALENKA
Illustrator

TOM STAEBLER
Vice President,
Art Director,
Playboy Magazine

CATHLEEN TOELKE
Illustrator

PAUL DAVIS

Since the early 1960s Paul Davis's work has been seen in major magazines, on book jackets, posters, and record album covers here and abroad.

He heads his own design firm in New York and serves as art director for Joseph Papp's NY Shakespeare Festival, as well as for *Normal Magazine.* He has executed a 70-foot mural for the "Arcadia" restaurant in Manhattan.

He has received innumerable awards and medals and is a member of the Alliance Graphique Internationale, the AIGA, and the Society of Illustrators.

130
Art Director:
Publisher:
Award:

PAUL DAVIS
Joseph Montebello
Harper and Row
Gold Medal

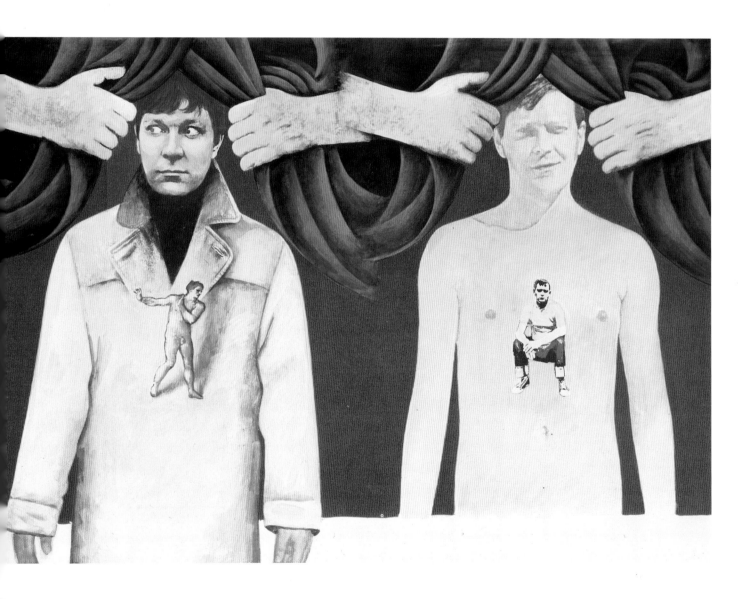

ROBERT GOLDSTROM

Goldstrom was born in Detroit to parents with artistic inclinations. They hoped and prayed that their son would become a doctor or lawyer. However, they have long since gotten over their shame and disappointment in his chosen profession and have even been known to show, say, a cover he painted for *The Atlantic* to their friends.

131   **ROBERT GOLDSTROM**
Art Director: Louise Fili
Publisher: Pantheon Books
Award: Silver Medal

JOHN H. HOWARD

Born in London in 1940, John Howard attended Camberwell School of Art, after which he worked as a librarian in the British Museum, taught painting, then became a full-time artist. Upon moving to New York in 1981 he began illustrating to subsidize his painting.

His clients include AT&T, CBS Records, Random House, Simon & Schuster, Condé Nast, *Forbes Magazine, Manhattan, inc., Life* and many others. His paintings have been exhibited in galleries both here and abroad.

132   **JOHN HOWARD**
Art Director: Tom Egner
Publisher: Avon Books
Award: Silver Medal

JOHN H. HOWARD

133   **JOHN HOWARD**
Art Director: Michael Mendelsohn
Publisher: Franklin Library
Award: Silver Medal

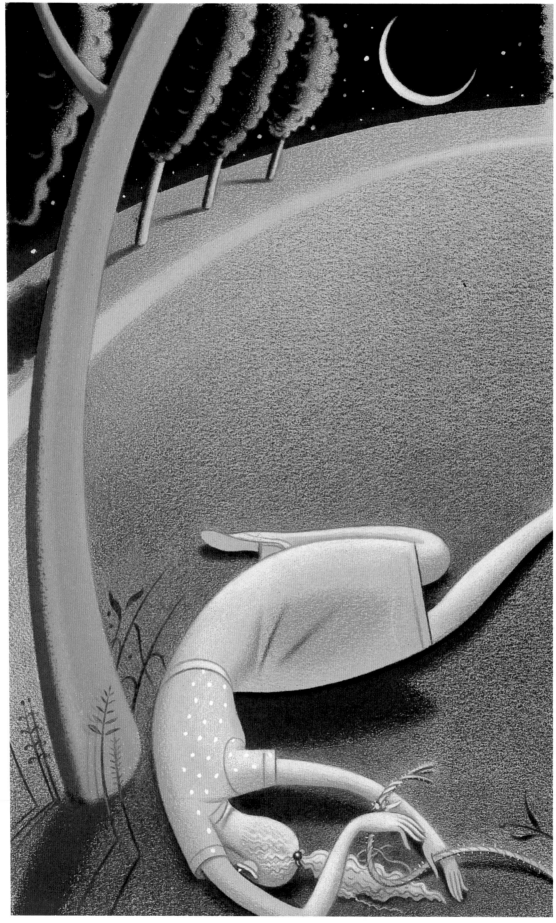

▲ 134   **DAVE CALVER**
Art Director: Tom Egner
Publisher: Avon Books

▶ 136 **BECKY HEAVNER**
Art Director: Cindy La Brecht
Publisher: Grove Press

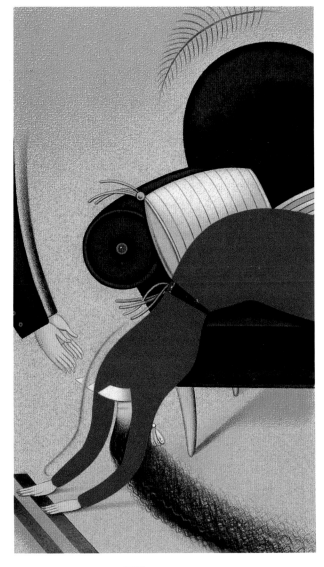

▲ 135 **DAVE CALVER**
Art Director: Tom Egner
Publisher: Avon Books

▶ 137 **RENEE KLEIN**
Art Director: Sara Eisenman
Publisher: Alfred A. Knopf

▶ 138   **HIRO KIMURA**
Art Director: Victor Weaver
Publisher: Dell Publishing

▼ 139   **JOYCE KITCHELL**
Art Director: Bonnie Schwartz
Client: Junior League of San Diego

▲ 140   PATRICIA
          ROHRBACHER

◀ 141   JONATHAN M. KNIGHT
Client: Florida Miniature Art
          Society

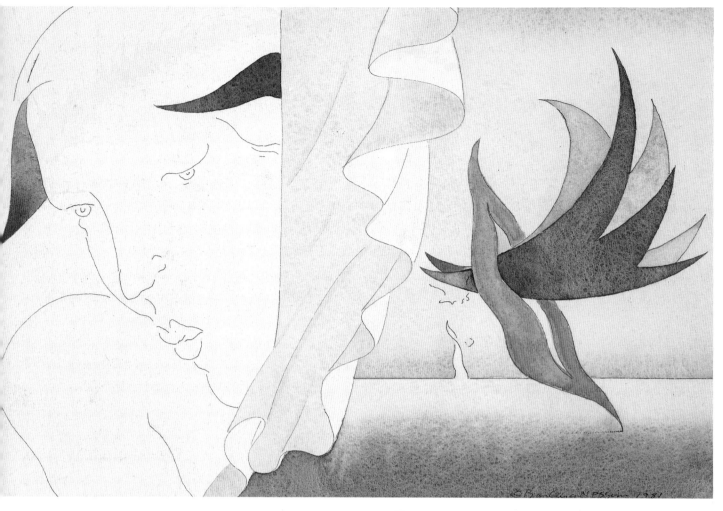

▲ 142 **BARBARA NESSIM**
Art Directors: Ruth Ross / Steven Diamond
Publisher: Fawcett/Ballantine Books

 143 **ART SPIEGELMAN**
Art Director: Louise Fili
Publisher: Pantheon Books

▲ 144 **MICHAEL MCCURDY**
Art Director: Trisha Hanlon
Publisher: Little, Brown and Company

▲ 145   MALCOLM T. LIEPKE

▶ 146   **DUGALD STERMER**
Art Director: Louise Fili
Publisher: Pantheon Books

▲ 147   **DUGALD STERMER**
Art Director: Louise Fili
Publisher: Pantheon Books

▲ 148   **ALAN E. COBER**
Art Director: Jennifer Dossin
Publisher: Franklin Library

▲ 149   **BRIAN AJHAR**
Art Director: Cheryl Asherman
Publisher: William Morrow

▲ 150   **MICHELLE BARNES**
Art Director: Sara Eisenman
Publisher: Alfred A. Knopf

▲ 151   **MARK PENBERTHY**
Art Director: Judy Loeser
Publisher: Vintage Books

▲ 152　**MARK PENBERTHY**
Art Directors: Greg Wilkin / Anna Demchick
Publisher:　Daw Books

▲ 153　**JOHN RUSH**
Art Director: Judy Loeser
Publisher:　Vintage Books

▲ 154　**JOHN RUSH**
Art Director: Judy Loeser
Publisher:　Vintage Books

▲ 155   **JOANIE SCHWARZ**
Art Director: Cindy La Brecht
Publisher: Grove Press

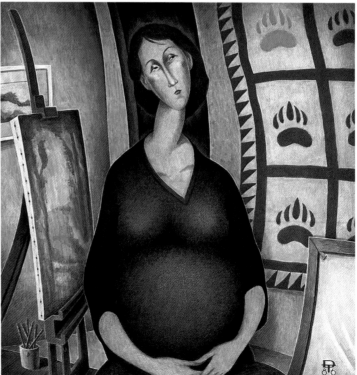

▶ 156   **DAVID TAMURA**
Art Director: Joseph Montebello
Publisher: Harper & Row

▲ 157   **ANTHONY RUSSO**
Art Director: Andy Carpenter
Publisher: St. Martin's Press

▶ 159 **DAVID FRAMPTON**
Art Director: Soren Noring
Publisher: Reader's Digest

▲ 158 **PAUL DAVIS**
Client: Methuen London Limited

▶ 160 **ROBERT VAN NUTT**
Art Director: Susan Mitchell
Publisher: Vintage Books

▲ 161 **PAUL DAVIS**
Art Director: Jackie Merri Meyer
Publisher: Warner Books

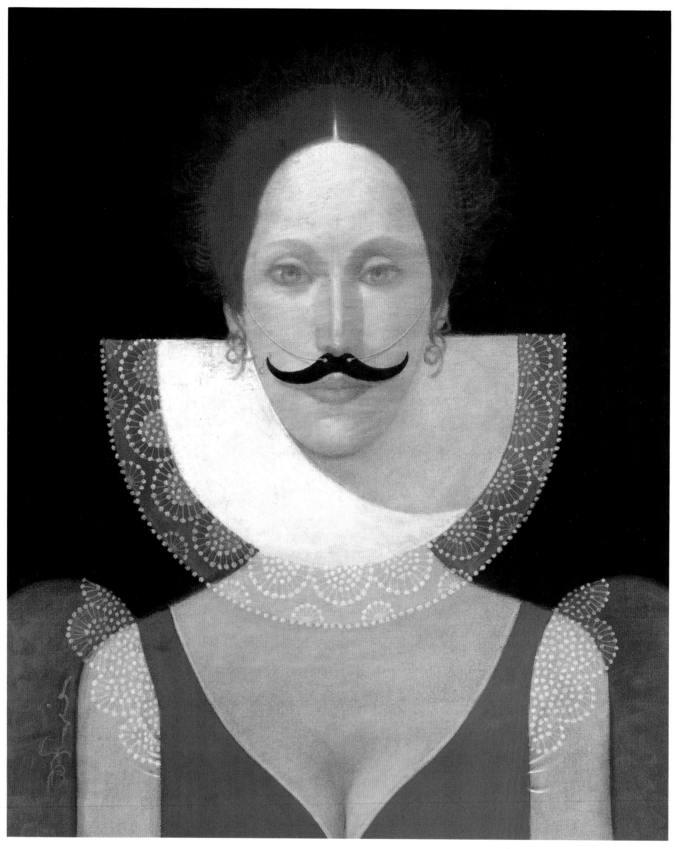

▲ 162   **MARK ENGLISH**
Art Director: Jim Plumeri
Publisher: Bantam Books

◀ 163   **MARK ENGLISH**
Art Director: Jim Plumeri
Publisher: Bantam Books

◀ 164   **MARK ENGLISH**
Art Director: Jim Plumeri
Publisher: Bantam Books

▲ 165   **MARIA RUOTOLO**

▲ 166   **ED LINDLOF**
Art Director: George Lenox
Publisher: University of Texas Press

◀ 167   **VIVIENNE FLESHER**
Art Director: Keith Sheridan
Client: Vintage Library

▲ 168   **TOM CURRY**
Art Director: Cheryl Asherman
Publisher: William Morrow Company

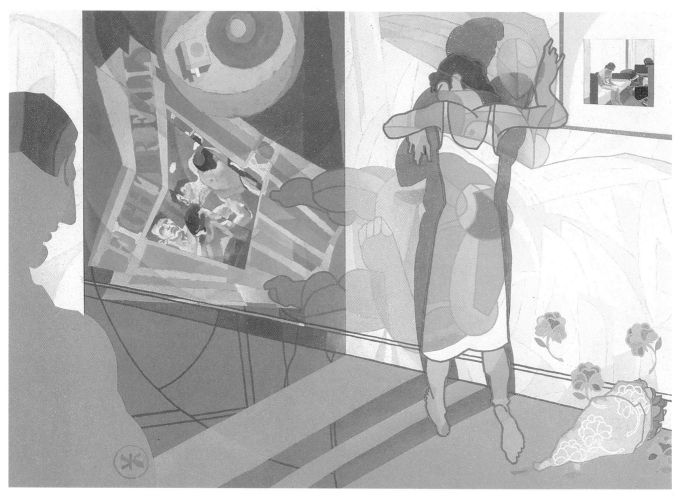

▲ 169 **VINCENT X. KIRSCH**
Art Director: Nancy Etheredge
Client: E. P. Dutton

▶ 170 **SARA SCHWARTZ**
Art Director: Joe Montebello
Publisher: Harper & Row

▲ 171   **AMANDA WILSON**
Art Director: Lee Wade
Publisher: Scribner's

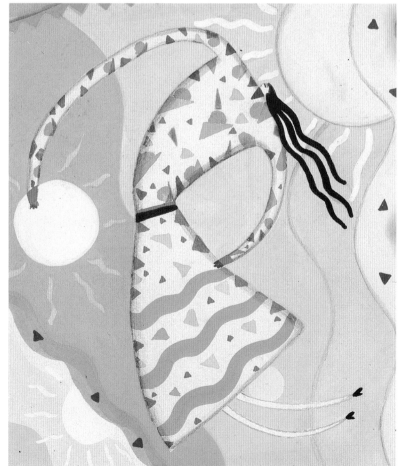

◀ 172   **KAREN KATZ**
Art Director: Joseph Montebello
Publisher: Harper & Row

▲ 173   **ED LINDLOF**
Art Director: Frederick Barthelme
Publisher: Mississippi Review

▲ 174   **DANIEL TORRES**
Art Director: Victor Weaver
Client: Dell Publishing Co. Inc.

▶ 175   **CARTER GOODRICH**
Art Director: Tasha Hall
Publisher: Alfred A. Knopf

▲ 176   **BEN PERINI**
Art Directors: Frank Kozelek / Tony Greco
Publisher: Berkley Publishing

▲ 177 **DOUGLAS FRASER**
Art Director: Lee Wade
Publisher: Macmillan

◄ 178 **DOUGLAS FRASER**
Art Director: Sara Eisenman
Publisher: Alfred A. Knopf

▲ 179   **JOHN NICKLE**
Art Director: Jamie Warren
Publisher: Bantam Books

▶ 180   **JOHN SPOSATO**
Art Director: Nancy Etheredge
Publisher: E. P. Dutton

▲ 181   **JUDY PEDERSEN**
Art Directors: Jackie Merri Meyer / Harold Nolan
Publisher: Warner Books

▲ 182   **JUDY PEDERSEN**
Art Director: Louise Fili
Publisher: Pantheon Books

▲ 183   **GORDON JOHNSON**
Art Director: Tom Egner
Publisher: Avon Books

▲ 184   **JOHN HOWARD**
Art Director: Cindy La Brecht
Publisher: Grove Press

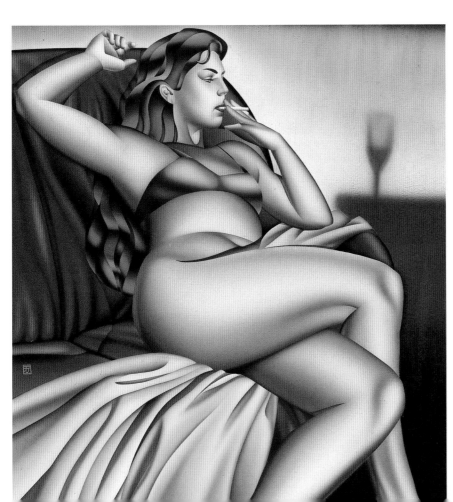

◄ 185   **JOHN JINKS**
Art Director: Krystyna Skalski
Publisher: Bantam Books

▲ 186   **STEVE GUARNACCIA**
Art Director: Joseph Montebello
Publisher: Harper & Row

▲ 187   **STEVE GUARNACCIA**
Art Director: Joseph Montebello
Publisher: Harper & Row

▶ 188   **STEVE GUARNACCIA**
Art Director: Joseph Montebello
Publisher: Harper & Row

▲ 189   **FRED MARCELLINO**
Art Director: Neil Stuart
Publisher: Viking Penguin Inc.

▲ 190   **WILSON MCLEAN**
Art Director: Frank Metz
Client: Simon & Schuster

▶ 191   **MARC TAUSS**
Art Director: Judy Loeser
Client: Vintage Contemporaries

▲ 192   **PETRA MATHERS**
Art Director: Constance Fogler
Publisher: Harper & Row

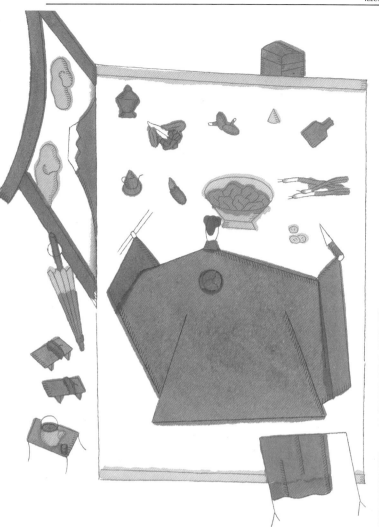

◀ 193   **PHILIPPE WEISBECKER**
Art Director: Louise Fili
Publisher: Pantheon Books

▲ 194   **PHILIPPE WEISBECKER**
Art Director: Sara Eisenman
Publisher: Alfred A. Knopf

◀ 195   **PHILIPPE WEISBECKER**
Art Director: Louise Fili
Publisher: Pantheon Books

◀ 196 **MELANIE MARDER PARKS**
Art Director: Louise Fili
Publisher: Pantheon Books

▼ 197 **DIANE DILLON / LEO DILLON**
Art Director: Trisha Hanlon
Publisher: Little, Brown and Company

▶ 198   **DAN REED**
Art Director: Joseph Montebello
Publisher: Harper & Row

▶ 199   **DAN REED**
Art Director: Joseph Montebello
Publisher: Harper & Row

▲ 200   **OREN SHERMAN**
Art Director: Jackie Merri Meyer
Publisher: Warner Books

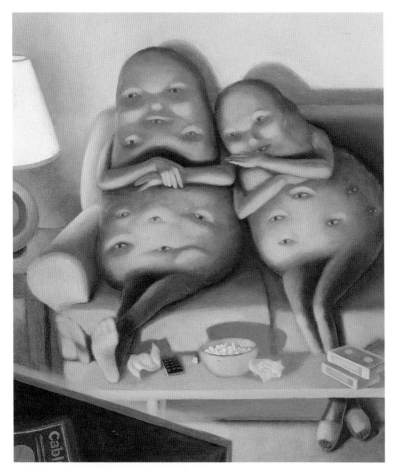

◀ 201   KIM DREW

▲ 202   **GARY KELLEY**
Art Director: Krystyna Skalski
Publisher: Bantam Books

▲ 203   **ERIC DINYER**
Art Director: Dorothy Wachtenheim
Publisher: Arbor House

▲ 204 **ANDRZEJ DUDZINSKI**
Art Director: Krystyna Skalski
Publisher: Bantam Books

▲ 205   **BRITT TAYLOR
          COLLINS**
Art Director: Britt Taylor Collins
Publisher: Multnomah Press

▶ 206   **HAYES HENDERSON**
Art Directors: Hayes Henderson /
                Arnold Gambill
Client: Rebel Art Magazine

▲ 207   **SCOTT JACKSON**
Art Director: Tom Egner
Publisher: Avon Books

▲ 208   DAVID SHANNON
Art Director: Melissa Jacoby
Publisher: Viking Penguin, Inc.

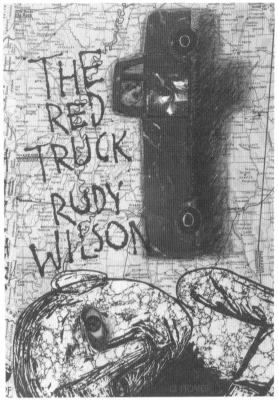

▲ 209 **DAVID SHANNON**
Art Director: Louise Fili
Publisher: Pantheon Books

▲ 210 **FRANCES JETTER**
Art Director: Sara Eisenman
Publisher: Alfred A. Knopf

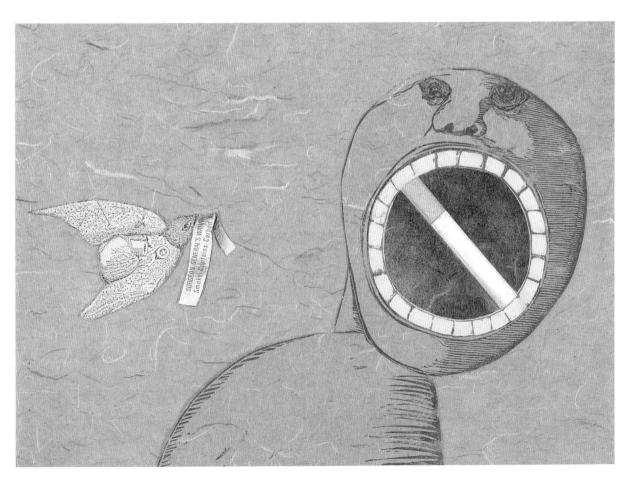

▲ 211 **FRANCES JETTER**
Art Director: Ginger Giles
Client: Franklin Watts, Inc.

▶ 213   **KENT WILLIAMS**
Art Directors: Archie Goodwin / Daniel Chichester
Client: Epic Comics

▲ 212   **DAVID SHANNON**
Art Director: Susan Mitchell
Publisher: Vintage Books

▶ 214   **COPIE**
Art Director: Cindy La Brecht
Publisher: Grove Press, Inc.

▲ 215   JANE COWLEY SZWED
Art Director: Mohamed Drisi

▲ 216   **RAFAL OLBINSKI**
Art Director: Neil Stuart
Publisher: Viking Penguin Press

▲ 217   **MICHEL GRANGER**
Art Director: Sara Eisenman
Publisher: Alfred A. Knopf

▲ 218   **KENT WILLIAMS**
Art Directors: Archie Goodwin / Daniel Chichester
Client: Epic Comics

▶ 219   **FRANK GARGIULO**
Art Director: Carin Goldberg
Publisher: Ferrar, Strauss & Giroux

▲ 220   **DAVID MONTIEL**
Art Director: Lee Wade
Publisher: Macmillan

◀ 221   **ROBERT CRAWFORD**
Art Director: Greg Wilkin
Publisher: New American Library

▲ 222   **ROBERT CRAWFORD**
Art Director: Greg Wilkin
Client: New American Library

◀ 223   **MICHAEL SCHWAB**
Art Director: Michael Vanderbyl
Client: American Institute of Graphic Arts

▶ 224   **DEBORAH HEALY**
Art Director: Joseph Montebello
Publisher: Harper & Row

▲ 225   **RICHARD AQUAN / STEPHEN ALCORN**
Art Director: Donald Munson
Publisher: Ballantine Books

▲ 226   **STEPHEN ALCORN**
Art Director: Doug Bergstreser
Publisher: Doubleday

▼ 227   **RUTH BAUER**
Art Director: Louise Noble
Publisher: Houghton Mifflin

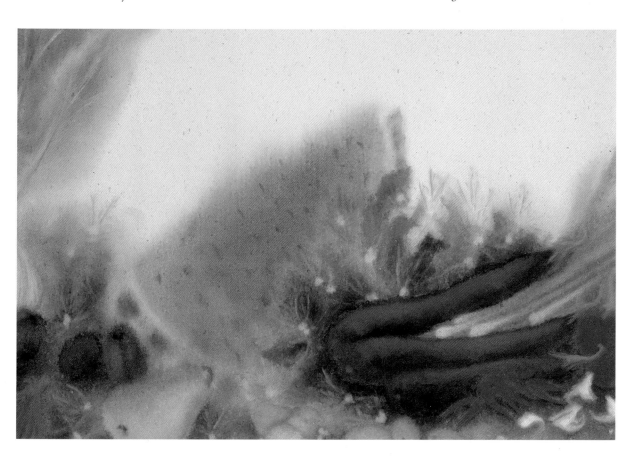

◀ 228   **ROBERT BURGER**
Art Director: Neil Stuart
Publisher: Viking Penguin, Inc.

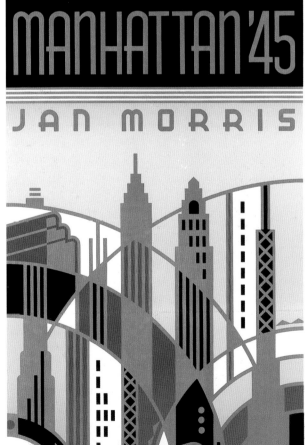

◀ 229   **DANIEL PELAVIN**
Art Director: Victoria Wong
Publisher: Oxford University Press

▶ 230   **MICHAEL PARASKEVAS**

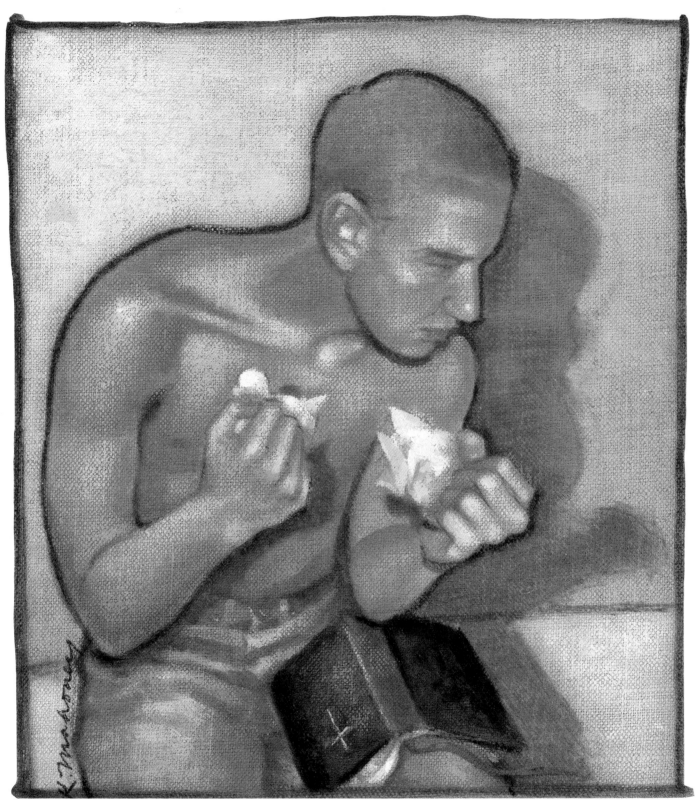

▲ 231   **KATHERINE MAHONEY**
Art Director: Klaus Schmidt
Client: Drei Eichen Verlag

◀ 232   **JOAN HALL**
Art Director: Keith Sheridan
Publisher: Random House

▲ 233   **JOHN COLLIER**
Art Director: Leslie Miller
Publisher: Bantam Books

◀ 234   **WINSLOW PINNEY PELS**
Art Director: Dorothy Wachtenheim
Publisher: Arbor House

▲ 235   ROB WOOD
Art Director: Dale Pollekoff
Publisher: Time-Life Books

▶ 236   HERB TAUSS
Art Director: Angelo Perrone
Publisher: Reader's Digest Condensed Books

▲ 237　**HERB TAUSS**
Art Director:　Angelo Perrone
Publisher:　　Reader's Digest Condensed Books

▲ 238   **MARK PENBERTHY**
Art Director: Beth Tondreau
Publisher: Thames & Hudson

▲ 239 **WENDELL MINOR**
Art Director: Al Cetta
Publisher: Thomas Y. Crowell

▲ 240 **WENDELL MINOR**
Art Director: Al Cetta
Publisher: Thomas Y. Crowell

▲ 241 **LESLIE BAKER**
Art Director: Trisha Hanlon
Publisher: Little Brown and Company

▲ 242 **LESLIE BAKER**
Art Director: Trisha Hanlon
Publisher: Little Brown and Company

▲ 243   **WENDELL MINOR**
Art Director: Vaughan Andrews
Publisher: Harcourt, Brace, Jovanovich

▶ 244   **BASCOVE**
Art Director: Louise Fili
Publisher: Pantheon Books

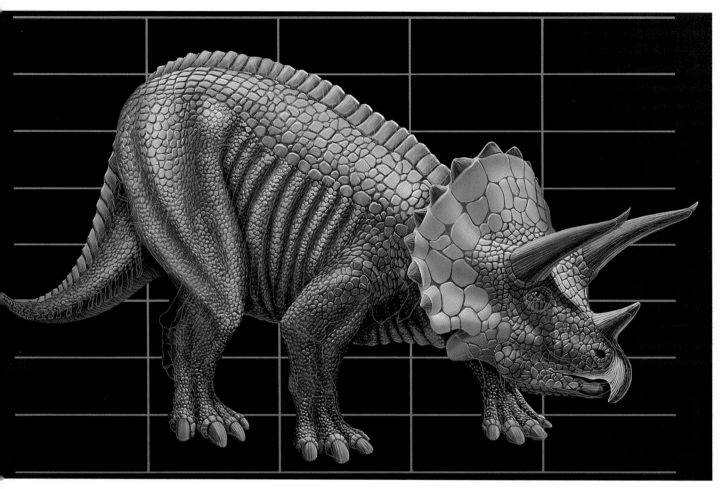

▲ 245   **EARL C. BATEMAN III**
Art Director: Earl C. Bateman III
Client: Celestial Arts

▶ 246   **SIMMS TABACK**
Art Director: Atha Tehon
Publisher: Dial Books

▲ 247   **PETER SIS**
Art Director: Denise Cronin
Publisher: Alfred A. Knopf

▶ 249   **MARSHALL ARISMAN**
Art Director: Gene Mydlowski
Publisher: Berkley Publishing

▲ 248   **TOM HALLMAN**
Art Director: Paolo Pepe
Publisher: Paperjacks, Ltd.

▶ 250   **CARTER GOODRICH**
Art Director: Krystyna Skalski
Publisher: Bantam Books

▲ 251 **PAT ALEXANDER**
Art Director: Jim Plumeri
Publisher: Bantam Books

▶ 252 **MICHELLE BARNES**
Art Director: Carin Goldberg
Publisher: Simon and Schuster

▲ 253 **JERRY PINKNEY**
Art Director: Atha Tehon
Publisher: Dial Books

▼ 254 **JERRY PINKNEY**
Art Director: Atha Tehon
Publisher: Dial Books

▲ 255   **JERRY PINKNEY**
Art Director: Al Cetta
Client: Harper & Row Publishers

▲ 256   **VERA ROSENBERRY**
Art Director: Gayla Goodell
Publisher: McgGraw-Hill School Division

◀ 257   **KENT WILLIAMS**
Publisher: Viking Penguin, Inc.

▲ 258   **DEREK JAMES**
Art Director: Ruth Ross
Publisher: Ballantine Books

◀ 259   **ROBERT GOLDSTROM**
Art Director: Tom Egner
Publisher: Avon Books

▲ 260   **MEL ODOM**
Art Director: Jamie Warren
Publisher: Bantam Books

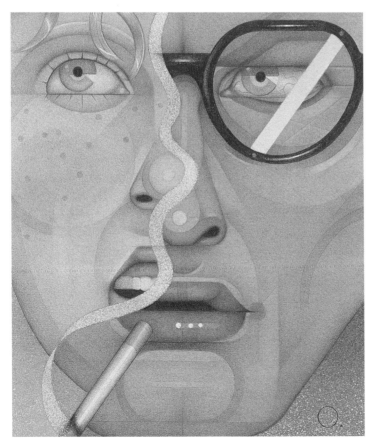

▲ 262   **MEL ODOM**
Art Director: Victor Weaver
Publisher: Dell Publishing, Inc.

◄ 261   **MEL ODOM**
Art Director: Louise Fili
Publisher: Pantheon Books

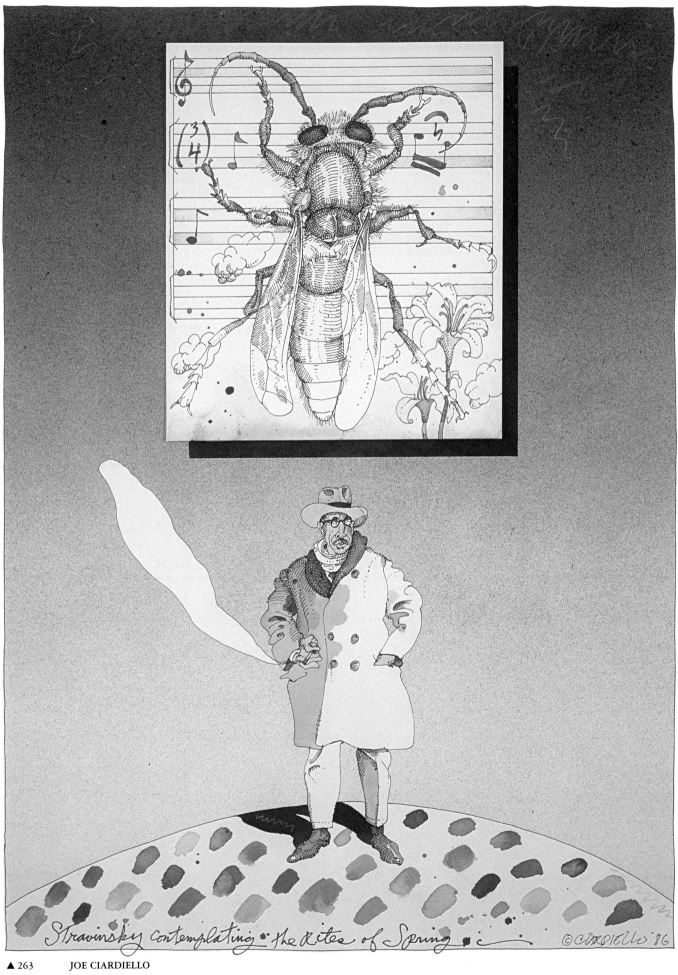

Stravinsky contemplating the Rites of Spring ©Ciardiello '86

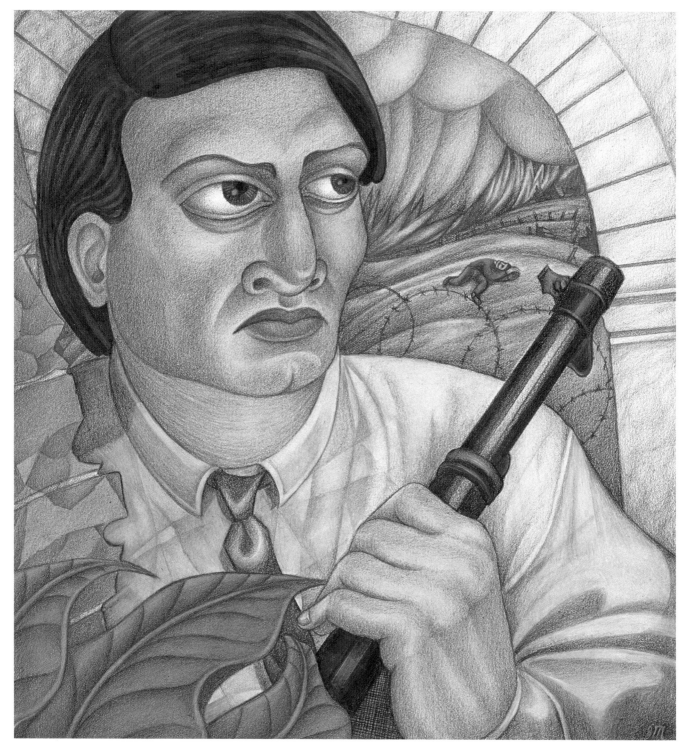

▲ 264   **JILL MCELMURRY**
Art Directors: Judy Loeser / Keith Sheridan
Publisher: Vintage Books

▲ 265   **JIM DIETZ**
Art Director: David Tommasino
Publisher: Scholastic, Inc.

◄ 266   **LISA FALKENSTERN**
Art Director: Jackie Merri Meyer
Publisher: Warner Books

Award Winners

Advertising

GOLD MEDAL

Edward S. Gazsi

GOLD MEDAL

John K. Hom

SILVER MEDAL

Bernie Fuchs

SILVER MEDAL

Bill Mayer

SILVER MEDAL

James McMullan

Jury

SHANNON STIRNWEIS
Chairman
Illustrator

GUY BILLOUT
Illustrator

H. TOM HALL
Illustrator

KEN KENDRICK
Art Director,
Wells, Rich, Greene

GARY PANTER
Illustrator

DAN SCHWARTZ
Illustrator

CHRIS SPOLLEN
Illustrator

EDWARD S. GAZSI

Born in 1944 in Trenton, New Jersey, Edward Gazsi studied art at Trenton Junior College, Brooklyn College, and Cooper Union where he received a B.F.A.

His illustrations have been done primarily for pharmaceutical advertising agencies and have appeared regularly in national periodicals.

Gazsi is presently on the teaching staff of Mercer County Community College and is frequently called upon to give lectures and demonstrations.

267
Art Director: George Courides
Agency: Thomas G. Ferguson Associates, Inc.
Client: Warner-Lambert Company
Award: Gold Medal

EDWARD S. GAZSI

JOHN K. HOM

After graduating at the top of his class from Art Center College of Design, John Hom and his brother started their own illustration and design firm.

Their clients include IBM, AT&T, CBS, NBC, Walt Disney and Panasonic, to name a few.

Hom has received honors from *CA* magazine, *American Illustration,* and the Society of Illustrators in Los Angeles and New York.

268
Art Director: David Mocarski
Client: American Ballet Theatre
Award: Gold Medal

JOHN HOM

BERNIE FUCHS

After graduating from Washington University School of Fine Arts in St. Louis, Fuchs joined New Center Studio in Detroit, and in 1958 moved East with his family.

In the ensuing years he was named "Artist of the Year," won the Hamilton King Award, and had his work accepted for every Society of Illustrators Annual Exhibition since its inception in 1959.

In 1975 Fuchs was elected to the Society of Illustrators Hall of Fame, the youngest artist ever to be so honored.

269
Art Director: Tom Clemente
Client: Newspaper Advertising Bureau
Award: Silver Medal

BERNIE FUCHS

BILL MAYER

Following graduation from the Ringling School of Art, Bill Mayer joined Atlanta's Graphic Group, then Whole Hogg Studios, and eventually began his own freelance business.

Amid a jungle of stuffed animals and a human skeleton in his home in Atlanta, Mayer has created illustrations for clients such as McDonald's, *Playboy*, Johnson & Johnson, U.S. Steel, Exxon, and IBM.

A versatile artist, he has won awards from *Graphis, CA, Print,* the One Show, *Humor,* and the Art Directors Club.

270   **BILL MAYER**
Art Director: Tom Sapp
Agency: Burton Campbell
Client: Ryder Truck Rental
Award: Silver Medal

JAMES McMULLAN

Born in 1934 in North China, James McMullan was educated in Asia, Canada, and the United States.

In the late '60s he was a member of Push Pin Studio and later did journalistic illustrations for many magazines, including *Sports Illustrated, Rolling Stone,* and *New York.* His work has received numerous awards, including the Society of Illustrators Gold and Silver Medals.

He is an instructor at the School of Visual Arts and is the principal artist for the Lincoln Center Theatre.

271
Art Director: Jim Russek
Agency: Russek Advertising
Client: Lincoln Center Theatre
Award: Silver Medal/Hamilton King Award

JAMES MCMULLAN

▲ 272   **SCOTT REYNOLDS**
Art Director: Joseph Montebello
Client: Harper & Row

◄ 273   **SCOTT REYNOLDS**
Art Director: Joseph Montebello
Client: Harper & Row

▲ 275 **WILLIAM HILLENBRAND**
Art Directors: William Hillenbrand / Keith Bollmer
Client: Cincinnati Regatta Committee

◀ 274 **WILLIAM HILLENBRAND**
Art Director: Barron Krody
Client: Cincinnati Regatta Committee

▲ 276　　NICK GAETANO
Art Director:　Charles Schmaltz
Agency:　　　Rainoldi Kerzner & Radcliffe
Client:　　　 Smith Kline Diagnostic Inc.

▲ 277   **BART FORBES**
Art Director: Clyde Steele
Agency: Leo Burnett Advertising
Client: Marlboro

▲ 278   **BART FORBES**
Art Director: Kevin Kuester
Client: Federal Express

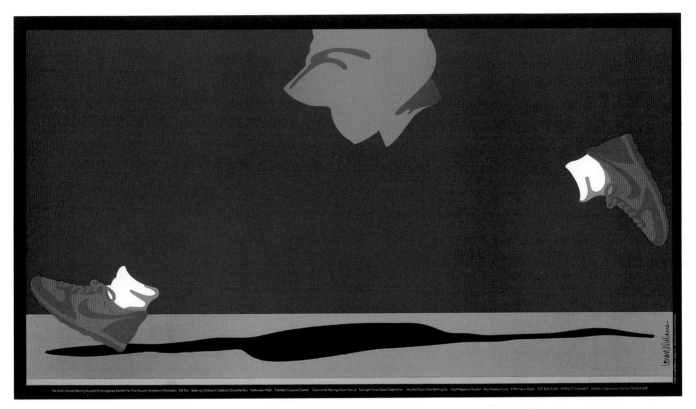

▲ 279   **ANDY DEARWATER**
Art Director: Lowell Williams
Client: Republic Bank Symphony Classic

▶ 280   **TERRY WIDENER**
Art Director: Michael Aron
Client: New York Magazine

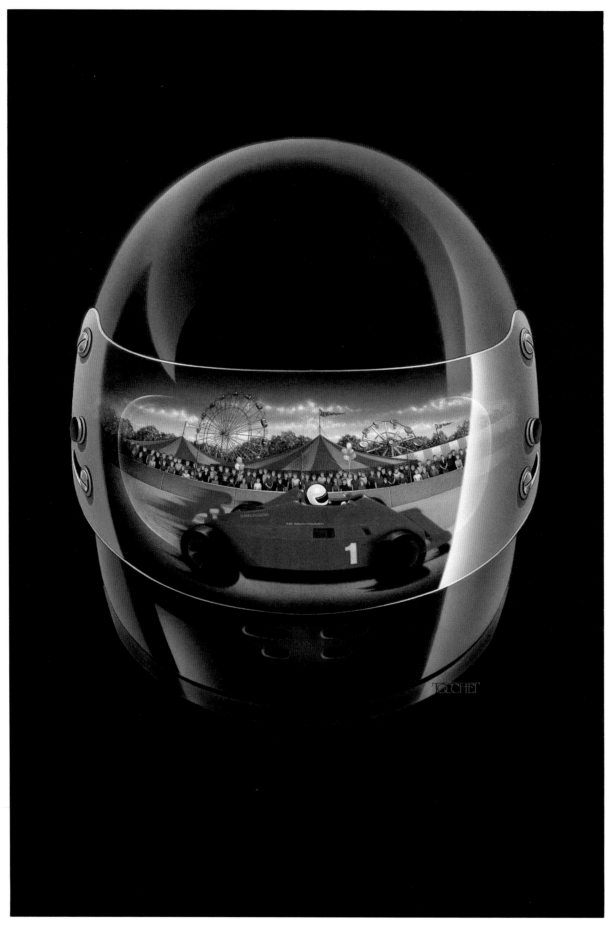

▲ 281   **MARK J. TOCCHET**
Art Director: Jowill Woodman
Agency: Advision
Client: Meadowlands Indy

▲ 282   GAYLORD WELKER

▲ 283   MURRAY TINKELMAN

▲ 284   BILL SIENKIEWICZ
Client: Epic Comics

▲ 285   BRIAN JEKEL

▲ 286   FRANCIS LIVINGSTON
Art Director: Christy Neal
Agency: Arias & Jarrall E
Client: Four Season Hotel

▲ 287   DARRYL ZUDECK
Art Director: Simon Bowden
Client: Ryder Cup

▲ 288   **GLENN HARRINGTON**
Art Director: Clyde Steele
Agency: Leo Burnett USA
Client: Philip Morris, Inc.

▲ 289   **VICTOR R. VALLA**
Client: Hankins and Tegenborg

▲ 290 **GRETCHEN HUBER**
Art Director: Stella Neves
Client: Freelance Exchange

◄ 291 **ALEX EBEL**
Art Director: Tom Bateman
Agency: Walker Associates
Client: Nissan

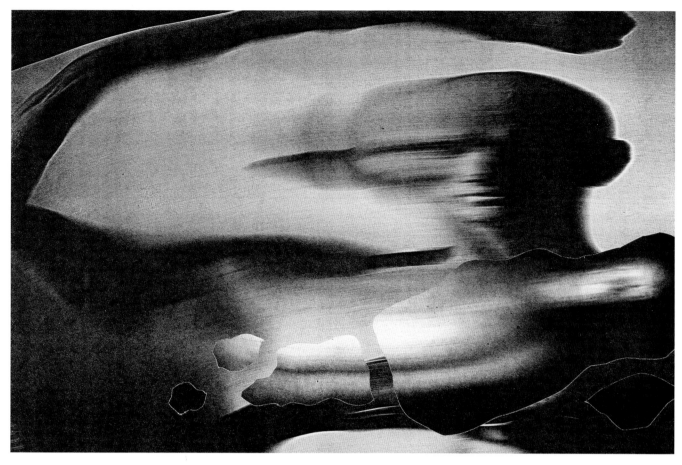

▲ 292   **GREGORY CANNONE**
Client: The Residents

▶ 293   **LESLIE WU**
Art Director: Leslie Wu
Client: Primary Project

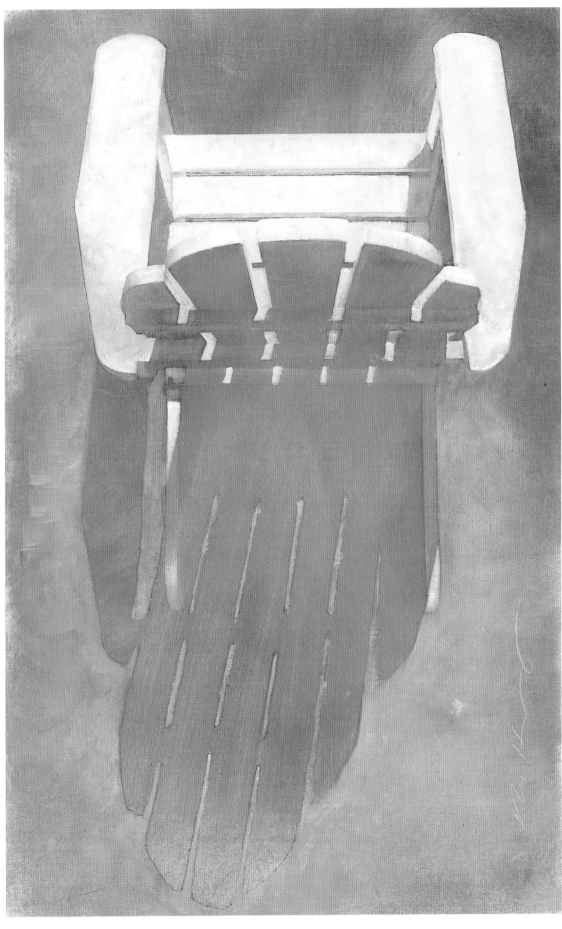

▲ 294   **ROBERT HUNT**
Art Director: Virginia Halstead
Agency: Eisaman Johns & Laws
Client: Pendelton Woolen Mills

▲ 295   **MARVIN MATTELSON**
Art Director: Tom Roth
Agency: Anderson and Lembke
Client: Plus Development Corporation

▲ 296   **IRWIN GREENBERG**

▲ 297   **JEFF SEAVER**
Art Director: Kay Crowson
Agency: J. Walter Thompson Company
Client: Northern Trust Bank

▲ 298   **EDWARD ABRAMS**
Art Director: Marvin Schwartz
Client: Capitol Records

▲ 299 **FREDERICK H. CARLSON**
Art Directors: Gary B. Reid / Dave Freeman
Client: County Records of Virginia

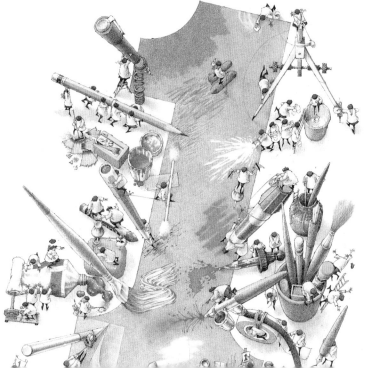

◀ 300 **JEFF SEAVER**
Art Director: Irwin Goldberg

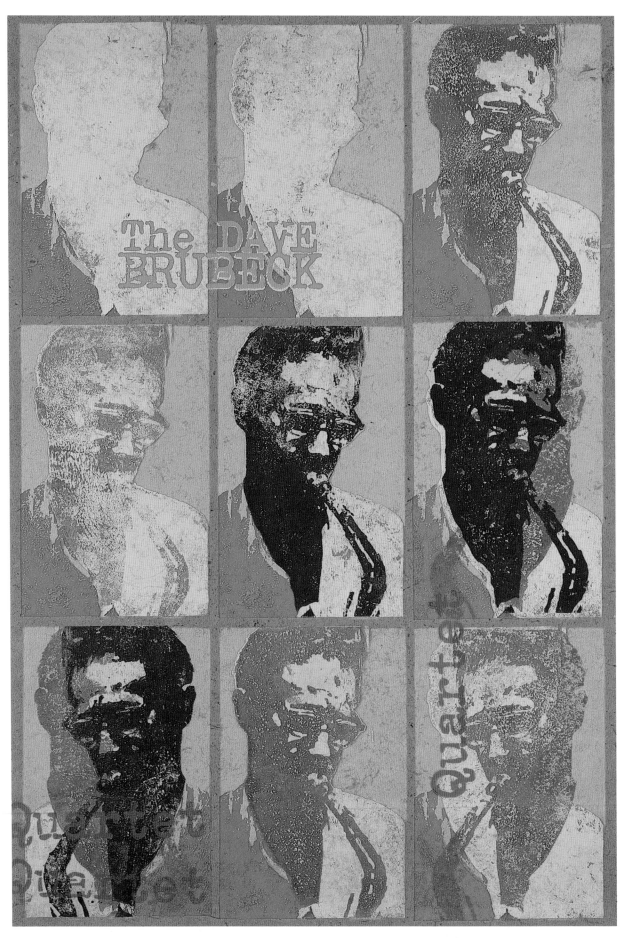

▲ 301   **JOHN HART**
Art Director: Sherri Nielsen

▶ 302 **JOHN HART**
Art Director: Sherri Nielsen

▶ 303 **GARY KELLEY**
Art Director: Joe Stelmach
Client: RCA Records

▲ 304 **GUY BILLOUT**
Art Director: Robert Miles Runyan
Client: Aspen Design Conference

▲ 305   **GARY KELLEY**
Client: Western Michigan University

▲ 306   **MICHAEL DAVID BROWN**
Art Director: Richard Sabean
Agency: BBD & O
Client: Kent/Lorillard Inc.

▲ 307   **MELISSA GRIMES**
Art Director: Ian Otway
Agency: Ted Bates Communications
Client: Benson & Hedges Mild 100'S

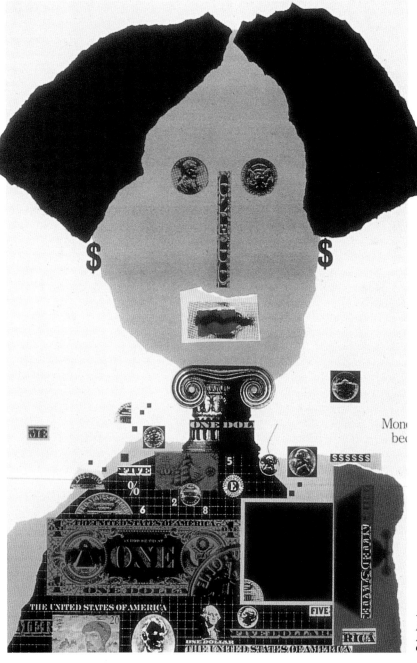

◄ 308   **MICHAEL DAVID BROWN**
Art Director: Gary Greenberg
Agency: Rossin Greenberg Seronick and Hill
Client: Boston Phoenix

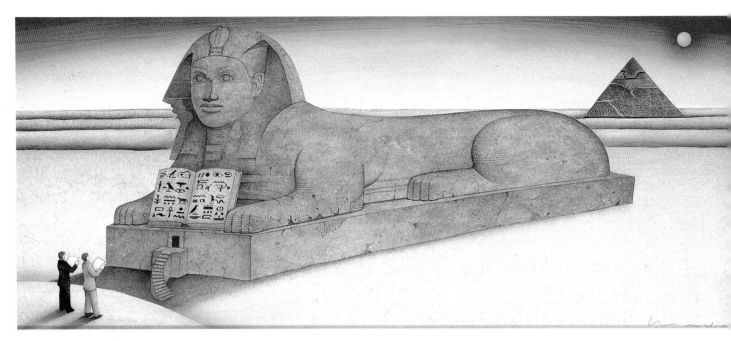

▲ 309   **JAMES ENDICOTT**
Art Director: Dennis Johnson
Client: Callaghan & Company

▼ 310   **CAMILLE PRZEWODEK**
Art Director: Andrew Danish
Client: Stanford Alumni Association

▲ 311   **KUNIO HAGIO**
Art Director: Robert Qually
Client: Crain Chicago Business

▲ 312   **JOHN THOMPSON**
Art Directors: Tom Demeter / Stavros Cosmopulos
Agency: Cosmopulos, Crowley & Daly, Inc.
Client: Allendale Insurance Company

▲ 313   **JOHN THOMPSON**
Art Director: Jerry Demoney
Client: Mobil Mystery Theater

▲ 314   **MARK STEELE**
Client: 11th Annual Artist's Ball

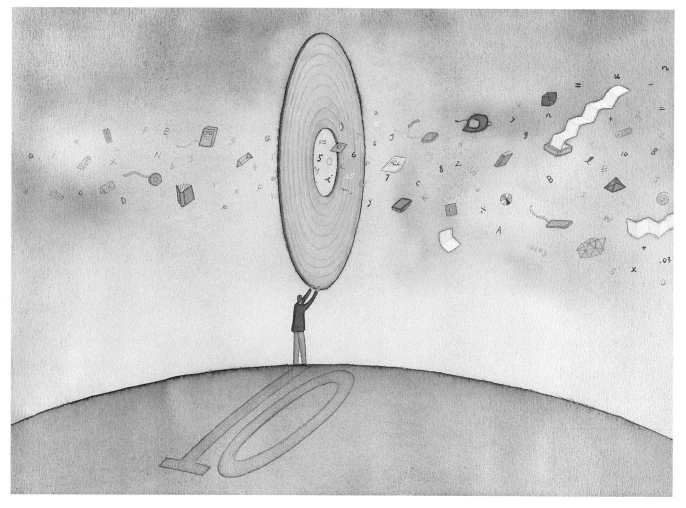

▲ 315 **LONNI SUE JOHNSON**
Art Director: Tom Hughes
Client: Lotus Development Corporation

▶ 316 **ARTHUR LIDOV**
Art Director: Myrtle Johnson
Agency: Ciba-Geigy Advertising
Client: Ciba-Geigy

▲ 317   **NORMAN WALKER**
Art Director: Jessica Weber
Client: M.C.I. Communications

▲ 318   **CHRIS HOPKINS**
Art Director: Chris Hopkins
Client: Zion

▲ 319   **JAMES E. TENNISON**
Art Director: Debra Branner
Client: Dallas Market Center

▶ 320   **M. JOHN ENGLISH**
Art Director: Debra Branner
Client: Dallas Market Center

▶ 321   **GARY RAHAM**

▼ 322   **ALEX MURAWSKI**
Art Director: David Bartels
Agency: Bartels & Carstens
Client: Budweiser

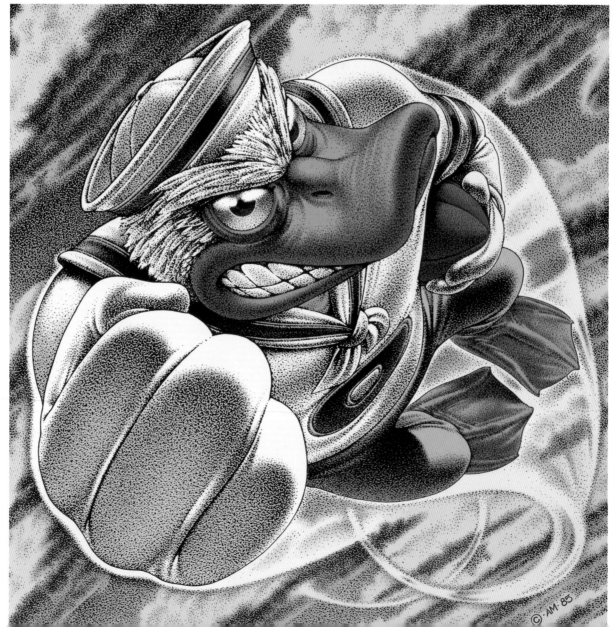

▶ 323 **RICHARD WEHRMAN**
Art Director: Bruce Keilar
Agency: Perri, Debes, Looney & Crane
Client: American Outdoor Footwear

▲ 325 **M. JOHN ENGLISH**
Art Director: Jim Paillot
Agency: Harmon-Smith, Inc.
Client: Hill's Pet Products, Inc.

◀ 324 **SID BINGHAM**
Art Director: Max Dunham
Client: L.A. Pet Food

▲ 326   **BERNIE FUCHS**
Art Director: Larry Corey
Agency: Richardson, Myers & Donofrio
Client: ICI Americas Inc.

▲ 327   **BERNIE FUCHS**
Art Director: Hank Quell
Agency: Tinsley Advertising
Client: Aberdeen Gold Club

▲ 328   **BERNIE FUCHS**
Art Directors: Vincent Travisano / Joann Giaquinto
Agency: Young & Rubicam
Client: A.T.&T

▲ 329   **JOEL POPADICS**
Art Director: Richard Mantel
Client: New York Magazine

▶ 330   **JOE ISOM**
Art Director: Fred Alvez
Client: Roche Laboratories

▲ 331   **IVAN CHERMAYEFF**
Art Directors: George Pierson / Gary Dueno
Client: HBO

◀ 332   **KAM MAK**
Art Director: Judith Sweeney
Agency: Sutter + Hennessey
Client: Stuart Pharmaceuticals

▲ 333 **DOUGLAS SMITH**
Art Director: Salvatore Sinare
Agency: Foote, Cone & Belding
Client: Pacific Telesis

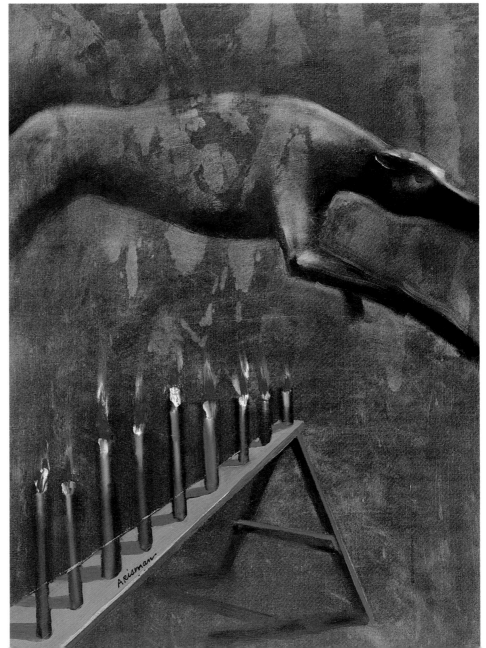

▶ 334 **MARSHALL ARISMAN**
Art Director: Silas Rhodes
Client: School of Visual Arts

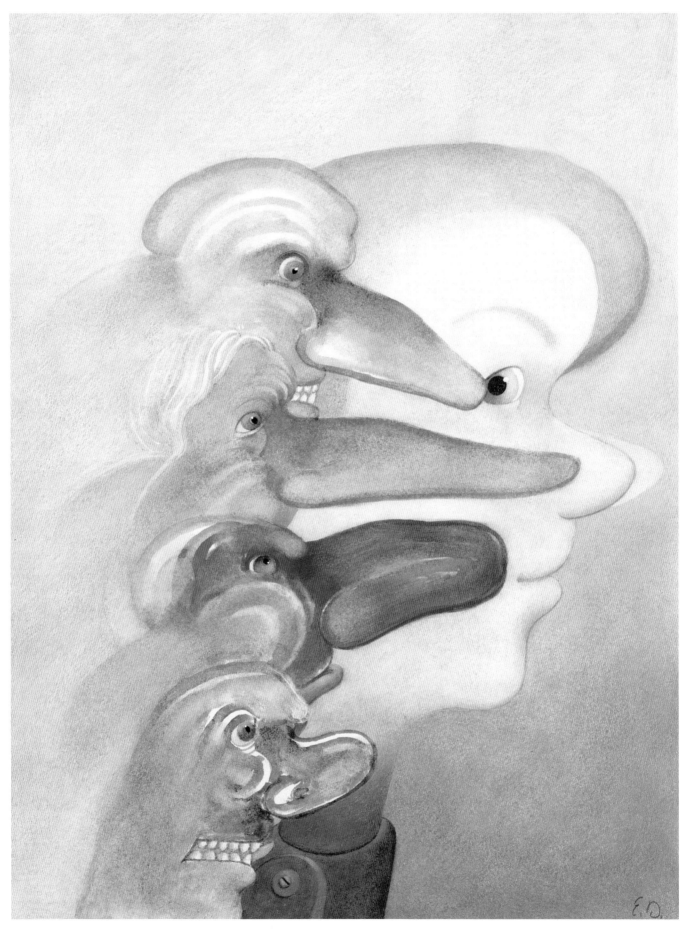

▲ 335   **ETIENNE DELESSERT**
Art Director: Rita Marshall
Client: Amstramgram Theater

▲ 336   **LINDA GIST**
Art Director: Leslie Hayes
Agency: Hayes + Associates
Client: Gore-Tex

▶ 337 **BRAD HOLLAND**
Art Director: Scott Woolsey
Agency: Shafer & Shafer
Client: Kendall Mcgraw Labs

▶ 338 **BRAD HOLLAND**
Art Director: Richard Lebenson
Client: RSVP

▲ 339   BRAD HOLLAND

▲ 341   **BILL MAYER**
Art Director: Lisa Doyle
Agency: Fahlgren & Swink
Client: Southern Company

▲ 340   **BILL MAYER**
Art Director: Lisa Doyle
Agency: Fahlgren & Swink
Client: Southern Company

▶ 342   **BILL MAYER**
Art Director: Nancy Rorabaugh
Agency: Pringle Dixon Pringle
Client: National Democratic
             Convention Committee

▲ 343   **BRALDT BRALDS**
Art Director: David Bartels
Agency: Bartels and Carstens
Client: Budweiser

▲ 344　　BRALDT BRALDS
Art Directors: David Bartels / Braldt Bralds
Agency:　　Bartels and Carstens
Client:　　　Budweiser

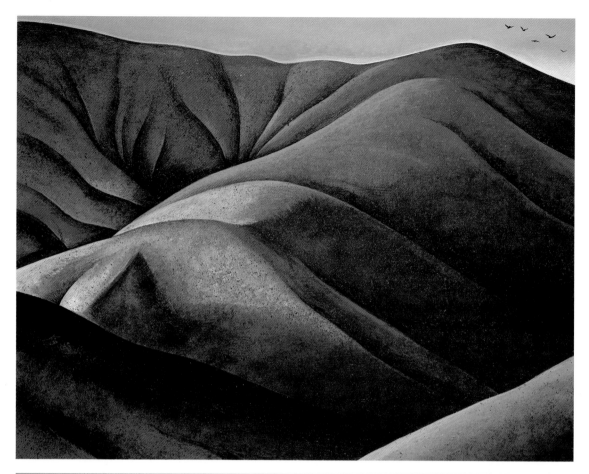

▲ 345   **WENDELL MINOR**
Art Director: Al Cetta
Client: Thomas Y. Crowell

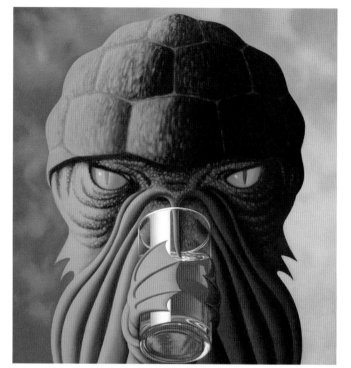

▲ 346   **BEN VERKAAIK**
Art Director: Frans Hettinga
Agency: PPGH/Moussault De Klencke 4
Client: De Melkunie

▲ 347   **BEN VERKAAIK**
Art Director: Peter Vos
Agency: Benton & Bowles Drentestraat
Client: Bavaria Bier

◀ 348   **GERRY GERSTEN**
Art Director: Bill Kerby
Agency: Lally, McFarland, Pantello
Client: Richardson, Vicks, Inc.

▲ 349   **RICK KRONINGER**

◀ 350   **GERRY GERSTEN**
Art Director: Catherine Flanders
Client: PC World

▲ 351   **MICHAEL GARLAND**
Art Director: Betsey Hitchcock
Client: Fortune 44

▶ 352   **DAN GOOZEE**
Art Director: Don Smolen
Client: Warner Brothers

▲ 353 **GEORGE STRICKLAND**
Art Directors: James Howe / Becky Benavides
Agency: Thompson-Marince Advertising
Client: San Antonio Festival

▶ 355 **LARRY MCENTIRE**
Art Director: Charles Webre
Agency: Sherry Matthews, Inc.
Client: Provident Development
Company

▶ 356 **CHARLES MCVICKER**

◀ 354 **BRALDT BRALDS**
Art Director: Cyndee Lamb
Agency: Campbell Mithun
Client: Control Data Corporation

▲ 357   PAUL CALLE / CHRIS CALLE

▲ 358   **WILSON MCLEAN**
Art Director: Tom Kane
Agency: Geer, Dubois Inc.
               Advertising
Client: B.A.S.F.

◄ 359   **GARY RUDDELL**
Art Director: Gene Mydlowski
Client: Campbell Woods

▲ 360 **BRIAN BAILEY**
Art Directors: Walter Bernard / Milton Glaser
Client: U.S. News and World Report

▶ 361 **CHARLES WATERHOUSE**
Art Director: Ralph A. Donnelly
Client: Confederate Marines

▶ 362 **JOHN A. MONTELEONE**

▲ 363 **ROBERT M. CUNNINGHAM**
Art Director: Stefan Strauss
Client: Martin Brinkmann AG

◀ 364 **ROBERT M. CUNNINGHAM**
Art Director: Gary Dueno
Client: HBO

▲ 365   ROBERT M. CUNNINGHAM
Art Director: Sam Bryan
Client: Continental Airlines

▲ 366   **KAZUHIKO SANO**
Art Director: Tony Lane Roberts
Agency: TLR & Associates
Client: Cineplex

▶ 367   **RICK MCCOLLUM**
Client: Retrovir

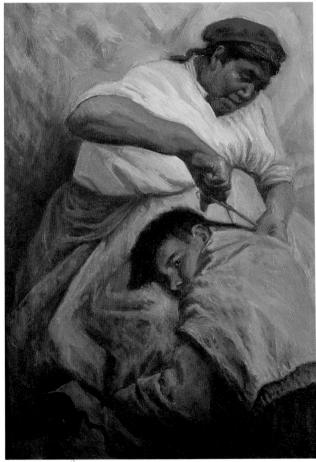

▲ 368   **MIRIAM LIPPMAN**
Client: Communication Arts Illustration
        Annual

▲ 369   **JOEL PETER JOHNSON**
Art Director: Joel Peter Johnson
Client: Buffalo Lyric Opera Theatre

▲ 370   **JOEL PETER JOHNSON**
Art Director: John Davis
Client: Buffalo News

▲ 371   **STEVEN ASSEL**
Art Director: Louie Youk
Client: Bantam Books

▲ 372   **JAMES MCMULLAN**
Art Director: Jim Russek
Agency: Russek Advertising
Client: Lincoln Center Theatre

◀ 373   **DAVID GROVE**
Art Director: David Reneric
Client: Manson Classics

▲ 374   **JAMES MCMULLAN**
Art Director: Masaaki Izumiya
Agency: Hakuho-Do Inc. Company
Client: Budweiser

▲ 375   **CHRIS SPOLLEN**

▲ 376   **KANG YI**
Art Director: Vince Robbins

▲ 377 **GERVASIO GALLARDO**
Art Director: Arnie Arlow
Agency: TBWA Advertising, Inc.
Client: Carillon Importers, Ltd.

▲ 378   JON ELLIS
Client: Welch's

▲ 379   MICHAEL SCHWAB
Art Director: Bill Merrikenl
Client: Perkins Shearer/Denver Symphony

▶ 380   JIM ANTHONY SALVATI
Art Director: Thomas H. Steele
Client: Hawaiian Express

▲ 381   MARK CASTELLITTO

▲ 382   **LAURA SMITH**
Art Director: Fern Bass
Client: New York Times

▶ 383   **TERESA FASOLINO**
Art Director: Marilyn Barnett
Client: Crabtree and Evelyn

▲ 384   **MARK HESS**
Art Director: Susan Casey
Agency: Anderson & Lembke

▲ 385   **JACK UNRUH**
Art Director: Rex Peteet
Client: International Paper Company

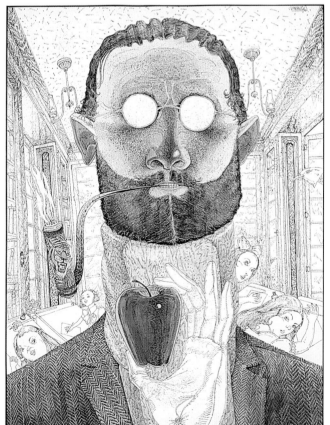

▲ 386   **BOB TILLERY / VAL TILLERY**
Art Directors: Bob Tillery / Val Tillery
Client: Dread Beat Records

◀ 387   **JACK UNRUH**
Art Director: Rex Peteet
Client: International Paper Company

▲ 388   **ROBERT HEINDEL**
Art Director: Ralph Schwartz
Agency: F. Scott Kimmich & Company
Client: Wyeth Laboratories

◀ 389   **MICHAEL GARLAND**
Art Director: Margery Peters
Client: Fortune Magazine

▲ 390   **PAUL DAVIS**
Art Director: Paul Davis
Client: New York Shakespeare Festival

▲ 391   **MICHAEL PARASKEVAS**
Art Director: Bob Defrin
Client: Atlantic Records

▲ 392   **MICHAEL PARASKEVAS**
Art Director: Bob Defrin
Client: Atlantic Records

▲ 393   **MICHAEL PARASKEVAS**
Art Director: Bob Defrin
Client: Atlantic Records

◄ 394   **BILL NELSON**
Art Director: Allen Weinberg
Client: CBS Records

▲ 395 **BILL NELSON**
Art Director: Allen Weinberg
Client: CBS Records

▶ 396 **DAHL TAYLOR**
Art Director: J. J. Stelmach
Client: RCA

▲ 397   **NANCY STAHL**
Art Director: Neil Pozner
Client: RCA-Bluebird

▲ 398 **NANCY STAHL**
Art Director: David Bender
Agency: Janklow Bender
Client: Le Tigre

▲ 399 **JOHN RUSH**
Art Director: Vidal Blankenstein
Agency: Maris, West + Baker
Client: Hughes Eastern Petroleum

▲ 400 **GARIN BAKER**
Art Director: Mario Jamora
Agency: Dorritie & Lyons
Client: Pfizer

▲ 401 **PAULA J. GOODMAN**
Art Director: Jim Nealey
Agency: Doyle, Graf, Mabley
Client: Marine Midland Bank

◄ 402 **MICHAEL MCCURDY**
Art Director: James Robertson
Client: Yolla Bolly Press

▲ 403   **C. MICHAEL DUDASH**
Art Director: Tom Vonderlinn
Client: Reader's Digest

◀ 404   **NEIL SHIGLEY**
Art Directors: Phil Gips / Kent Alterman
Client: HBO Pictures

▲ 405   **SCOTT SNOW**
Art Director: Chuck Penna
Agency: Penna Powers Cutting
Client: Pioneer Memorial
               Theatre

◀ 406   **FRANCESCO CLEMENTE**
Art Director: Christopher Austopchuk
Client: CBS Records

Award Winners

Institutional

GOLD MEDAL

Thomas Blackshear

SILVER MEDAL

C. Michael Dudash

SILVER MEDAL

Marco J. Ventura

Jury

**MIRIAM
SCHOTTLAND**
Chairman
Illustrator

JEFFREY CORNELL
Illustrator

MICHAEL DEAS
Illustrator

ALEX GNIDZIEJKO
Illustrator
and Portrait Painter

ROBERT McGINNIS
Illustrator

THEO RUDNAK
Illustrator

JIM SHARPE
Illustrator

CRAIG TENNANT
Illustrator

MARY ZISK
Art Director,
PC Magazine

THOMAS BLACKSHEAR

Upon graduating from the American Academy of Art in Chicago, Blackshear worked for Hallmark Cards for one year, then for God-bold/ Richter Studio, and in 1982 began freelancing.

He has produced illustrations for advertising, calendars, books, posters, and a series of U.S. postage stamps.

A winner of many awards, Blackshear also taught at the Academy of Art School in San Francisco.

407

THOMAS BLACKSHEAR II

Award: Gold Medal

C. MICHAEL DUDASH

Born in 1952 in Mankato, Minnesota, Michael Dudash majored in art at Macalester College in St. Paul, and at the Minneapolis College of Art and Design.

After serving as staff illustrator for McGraw-Hill, *Postgraduate Medicine* and *Sports Medicine* in Minneapolis, he be-gan freelancing out of his home in Warren, Vermont.

He has won numerous awards, and has taught an illustration class at Vermont Community College.

408
Award:

C. MICHAEL DUDASH
Silver Medal

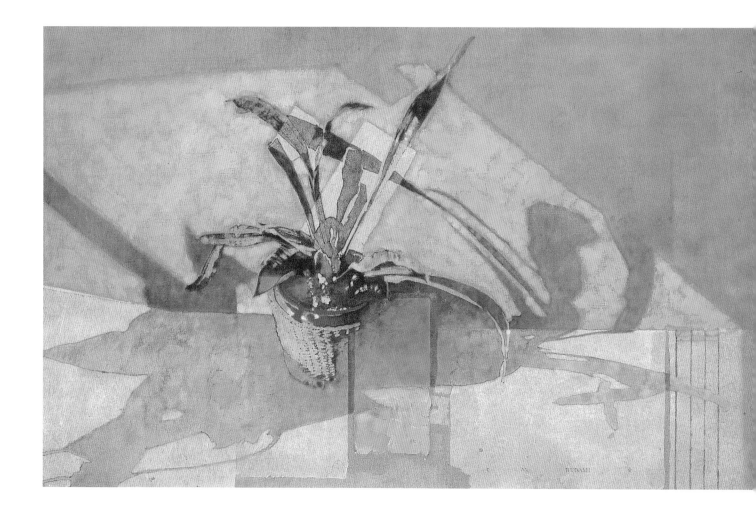

MARCO J. VENTURA

A native of Italy, Marco Ventura was born on May 20, 1963, in Milan. He attended the Accademia di Belle Arti di BRERA and later, the School of Visual Arts in New York.

Ventura is a member of a talented, artistic family; his father is a children's book illustrator and his brother is also an illustrator.

409
Art Director: Piero Ventura
Client: Arnoldo Mondadori
Award: Silver Medal

MARCO J. VENTURA

▲ 410 **PETER LISIESKI**
Client: Janice Wilhelm Fine Art

◀ 411 **PAUL ORLANDO**
Client: Maritz Motivation Inc.

▲ 412   **BEN VERKAAIK**
Client: Titanic

▲ 413   **BEN VERKAAIK**
Art Director: Henny Van Varik
Agency: Ggk Herengracht 392
Client: W.U.H.

▲ 414   **BOB BUCCELLA**   ▲ 415   **PATE MARTIN**

▲ 416   **JENNIFER HEWITSON**
Art Director: Brenda Bodney
Client: San Diego Zoo

▲ 417   **BRIAN AJHAR**
Art Director: Gregg Bernhardt
Agency: Bernhardt Fudyma
Client: Maxwell House

▲ 418   **TRACY W. LARSEN**
Art Director: Robert T. Barrett

▲ 419   **BILL MAYER**
Art Director: Rick Anwyl
Client: Bill Mayer

▲ 420   **ROBERT GRACE**

▲ 421   **ROBERT GRACE**
Art Director: Karen Malzeke-Mcdona
Client: Tabor Publishing

▲ 422　　　QUANG HO

▲ 423　　　**KRISTEN FUNKHOUSER**
Art Director:　Karl Bornstein
Client:　　　　Mirage Editions

▲ 424　　　**G. ALLEN GARNS**
Art Director:　Ken Curry
Agency:　　　　Mullen Advertising

▲ 426   **ROBERT HEINDEL**
Art Director: Philip Arnott
Client: Obsession of Dance Company

▶ 427   **ROBERT HEINDEL**
Art Director: Philip Arnott
Client: Obsession of Dance Company

◀ 425   **ROBERT HEINDEL**
Art Director: Philip Arnott
Client: Obsession of Dance Company

▲ 428 **KENN BACKHAUS**
Art Director: Kenn Backhaus
Client: Art Factory

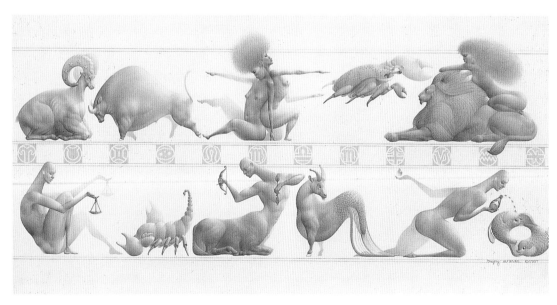

▲ 429 **GREGORY MCMICKIN**

▲ 430   **ROBERT MCGINNIS**
Client: Husberg Fine Arts Gallery

▲ 431   **ROBERT MCGINNIS**
Client: Husberg Fine Arts Gallery

▲ 432   **TOM NIKOSEY**
Art Director: Doug Morris
Agency: Grey Advertising
Client: Santa Anita Park

▲ 433   **FRANCIS LIVINGSTON**
Client: Freda Scott

▲ 434   **WILLIAM HILLENBRAND**
Art Director: William Hillenbrand
Client: Siboy Cline Realtor

▲ 435   **DONALD DEMERS**
Art Director: Francesca Mastrangelo
Client: HCA Portsmouth Regional Hospital

▲ 436   **BOB RUSSO**
Client: Habersham Group

▲ 437 **BRALDT BRALDS**
Art Director: Derek Ungless
Client: Eikelenboom-1988 Calendar

▲ 438   DAVID LEVINSON

▲ 439   DAVID GROVE
Art Directors: Richard Puder / Chris Spollen
Client: Society of Illustrators

▲ 440   SALLY WERN COMPORT
Art Director: Lisa Hill
Agency: Wood + Cohen
Client: Shands Hospital

▲ 441   **BART FORBES**
Art Director: Bill Duevell
Client: ABC Television

▲ 442   **BART FORBES**
Art Director: Jack O'Grady
Client: Jack O'Grady Studios

▲ 443 **BART FORBES**
Art Director: Cindy Ray
Client: Poster Place

▲ 444   **TOM CURRY**
Art Director: Gary Gibson
Client: Lotus Publications

▲ 445   **TOM CURRY**
Art Directors: Don Johnson / Paul Donchevsky
Agency: Johnson & Simpson Graphics
Client: Warner Lambert Company

▼ 447   **DUGALD STERMER**
Art Director: Louise Fili
Client: Pantheon Books

▲ 446   **CRAIG CALSBEEK**
Art Director: Craig Calsbeek
Client: Color Press

▲ 448   TIM O'BRIEN

▶ 449   **M. JOHN ENGLISH**
Art Director: Richard Korek
Client: Lubow Mckay Stevens and Lewis

▲ 450   **M. JOHN ENGLISH**
Art Director: Joanne Palulian
Client: American Showcase

▲ 451   **RAFAL OLBINSKI**
Art Director: Buck Smith
Agency: Hawthorne Wolfe
Client: Ralston Purina

▲ 452   **GEORGE Y. ABE**
Art Directors: Suzanne Tavernor / Gary Lacoma
Client: American Network

▲ 453 **CAMILLE PRZEWODEK**
Art Director: John Coll
Agency: Allen & Dorward, Inc.

▲ 454 **DONALD DEMERS**
Art Director: Francesca Mastrangelo
Client: HCA Portsmouth Psychiatric Pavillion

▲ 455 **BILLY O'DONNELL**
Art Director: Dave King
Client: Maritz Motivation Company

▶ 456 **DANIEL PELAVIN**
Art Director: Alicia Messina
Client: Ambassador Arts, Inc.

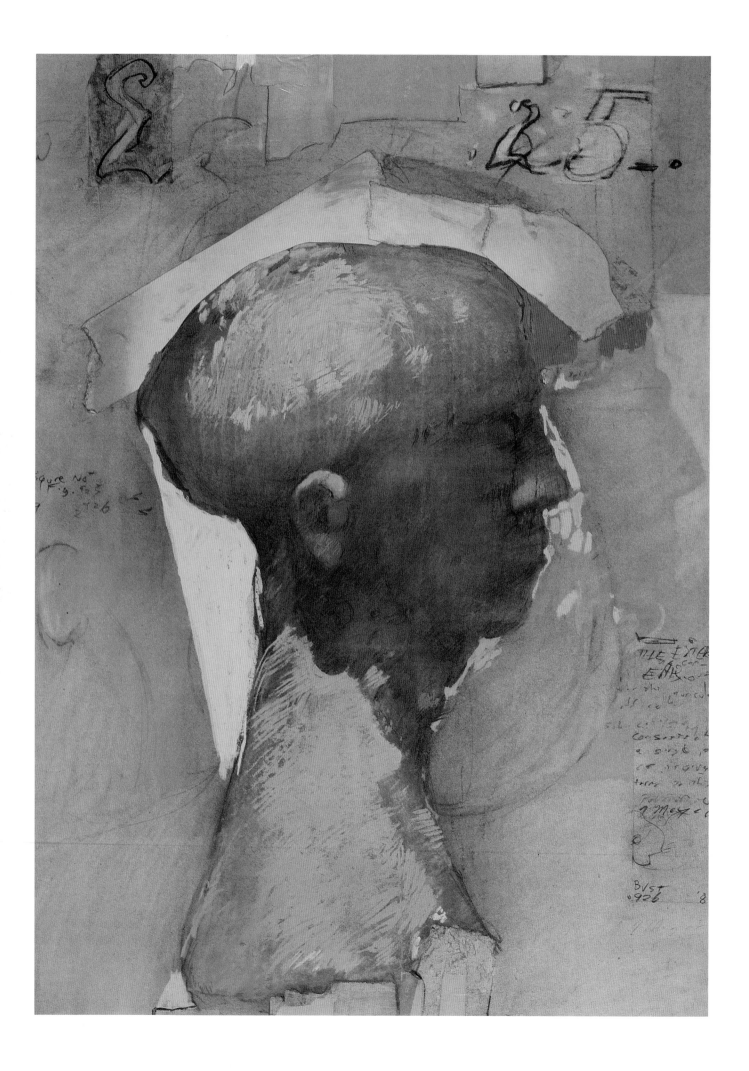

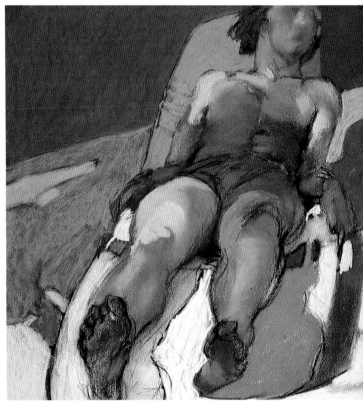

▲ 458   **JEFF MEYER**   ▲ 459   **JEFF MEYER**

◀ 457   **JEFF MEYER**

▲ 460   **BUD KEMPER**
Art Director: Curt Simpson
Client: Maritz Motivation Company

▶ 461   **BOB CONGE**
Art Director: Bob Conge
Client: Park Avenue Merchants Association

▲ 462   **BOB CONGE**
Art Director: Bob Conge
Client: Communicator of the Year Awards

▲ 463 **STEVE HEIMANN**
Art Director: Stephen Edelstein
Client: Sierra Leone Postal Service

▲ 464   **WILSON MCLEAN**
Art Director: Wilson Mclean
Client: Caribbean Photographic Co.

◀ 465   **ARDEN VON HAEGER**

▶ 466   **DAVID FISHMAN**
Art Director: Robin Gilmore Barnes
Client: School of Visual Arts

▶ 467   **MICHELE MANNING**
Art Director: Cynde Starck
Client: San Francisco Society of
               Illustrators

▲ 468   **GARY KELLEY**
Client: College Hills Art Festival

▲ 469 **MARK PENBERTHY**
Art Director: Suzanne Zumpano
Client: Prentice-Hall

MA KA TAI ME SHE KIA KIAK

▲ 470   **KIM BEHM**
Art Director: Duane Wood
Client: Cedar Arts Forum

▶ 471   **THOMAS BLACKSHEAR II**
Art Director: David Bartels
Agency: Bartels and Carstens
Client: Anheuser-Busch

▲ 472   KEVIN C. HAWKES

▶ 473   KEVIN C. HAWKES

▶ 474   **MARK A. FREDRICKSON**
Art Director: David Bartels
Agency: Bartels and Carstens
Client: David Bartels

▲ 475   **MARK A. FREDRICKSON**
Art Director: Chip Travers
Client: Tucson Balloon Fiesta

▲ 476   **JENNIFER HARRIS**
Art Director: Ted Karch
Agency: Beaird Agency
Client: Chili Society, Ltd.

▶ 477   **TED WRIGHT**
Art Director: Bill Wehrman
Agency: Maritz, Inc.
Client: Texas Beef Producers

▲ 478   **PAUL CALLE**
Art Director: Ellen Pedersen
Client: Mill Pond Press, Inc.

▲ 479   **BOB ZIERING**
Client: New York City Opera

▲ 480   **KENT WILLIAMS**
Client: Jack Meier Gallery/Allen Spiegel Fine Arts

▲ 481   **ROBERT HUNT**

▲ 482   **HODGES SOILEAU**
Art Director: John deCesare
Client: Society of Illustrators

▲ 483   **HODGES SOILEAU**
Client: GWS Gallery

▶ 484   **HODGES SOILEAU**
Client: U.S. Air Force

▲ 485   **DAVID KILMER**
Client: Sports Club of America

▲ 486   DAVID M. BECK

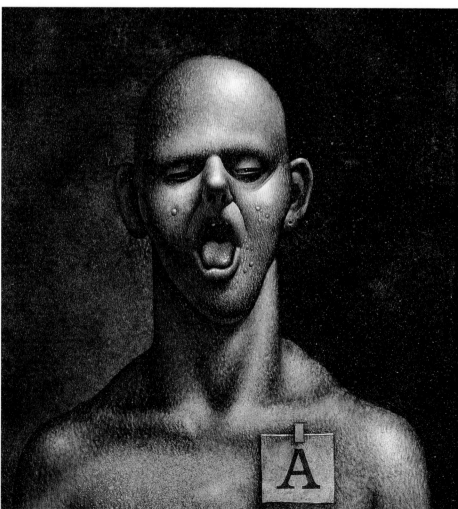

▶ 487   **JOHN JUDE PALENCAR**
Art Director: John Jude Palencar
Client: Byron Preiss Visual
               Publications

▲ 488   **JOHN JUDE PALENCAR**
Art Director: David Bartels
Agency: Bartels and Carstens
Client: Anheuser-Busch

▲ 489 **MICHAEL DAVID BROWN**
Art Director: Michael David Brown
Client: Winterberry Publishing

▼ 491 **FRAN VUKSANOVICH**

▲ 490 **MICHAEL DAVID BROWN**
Art Director: Michael David Brown
Client: Winterberry Publishing

▲ 492   FRAN VUKSANOVICH

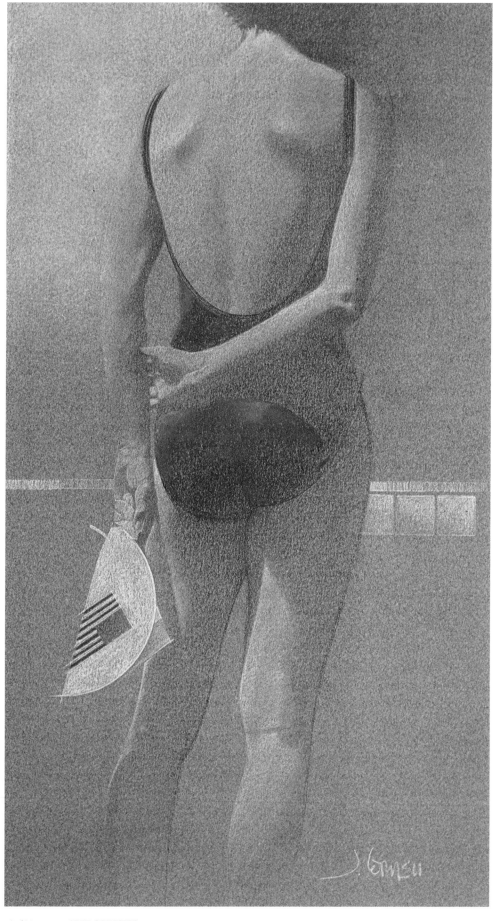

▲ 493   **JEFF CORNELL**
Art Director: Jeff Cornell
Client: Artco

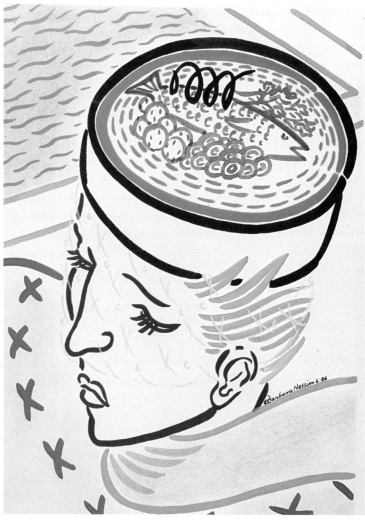

▲ 494   **JEFF CORNELL**
Art Director: Jeff Cornell
Client: Artco

▲ 495   **BARBARA NESSIM**

▲ 496   **SHELDON GREENBERG**

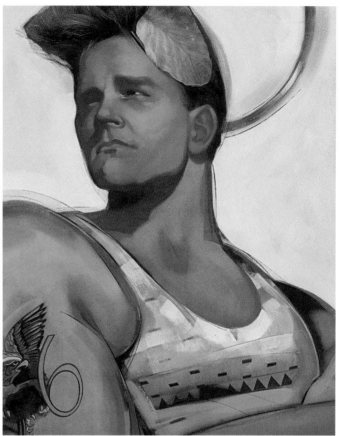

▼ 497   **SUZANNE BARNES**

▲ 498   **DEBRA WHITE**
Art Director: Edward Booth-Clibborn
Client: American Illustration

▶ 499   **BURRELL DICKEY**
Art Director: Vernon Head
Agency: Rauh, Good, Darlo &
              Barnes, Inc.
Client: San Jose Convention &
              Visitors Bureau

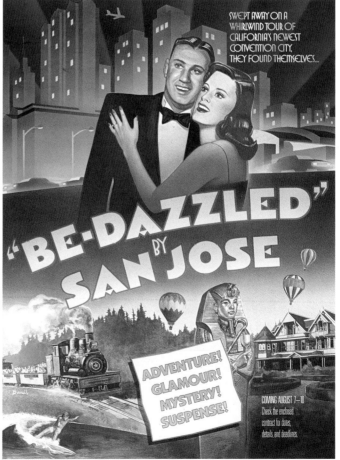

▼ 500   JAMES E. TENNISON

▲ 501   **MALCOLM T. LIEPKE**
Art Director: Martin Pederson
Client: Vis, Inc.

▲ 502   **MALCOLM T. LIEPKE**
Art Director: Martin Pederson
Client: Vis, Inc.

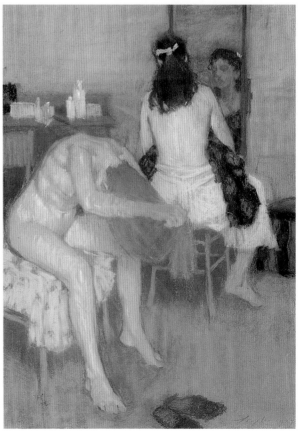

▶ 503   **MALCOLM T. LIEPKE**

▲ 504   **DOUGLAS FRASER**
Art Director: Sherry Charles
Agency: J. Walter Thompson
Client: City of San Francisco

▲ 505   **FRANK RICCIO**
Art Director: Richard Lebenson
Client: E & F Construction Company

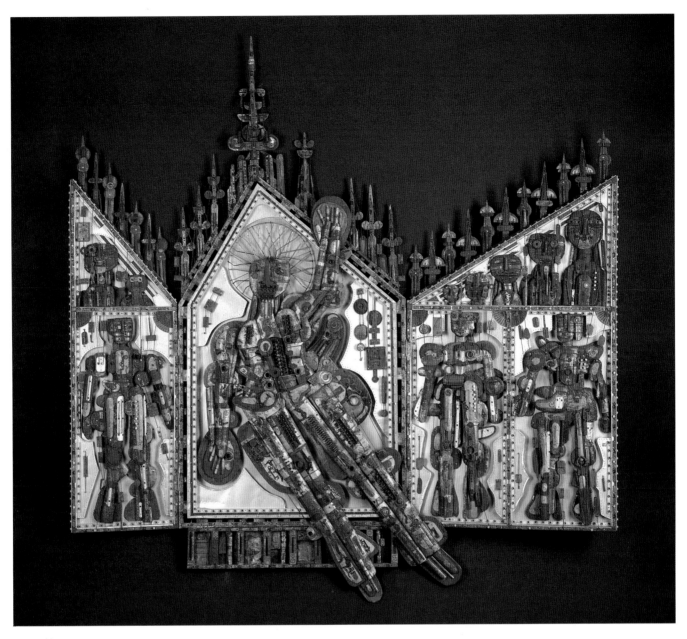

▲ 506   **EUGENE HOFFMAN**
Client: Museum of Natural History

▲ 507   **TERESA FASOLINO**
Art Director: Karen Brown
Client: Dayton Stores

▼ 508　　**JUDY PEDERSEN**
Art Director:　Debbie Rausbaum

▲ 509　　　**TERRY HOFF**

▲ 510　　　**JANE STERRETT**

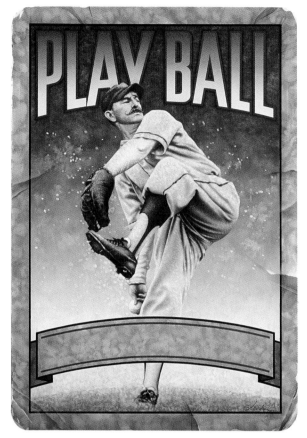

▲ 511   **BRIAN SHERIDAN**
Art Director: Brian Sheridan
Client: Castle Gallery/College of New Rochelle

▲ 512   **M. CHANDLER MARTYLEWSKI**

▲ 513   **DAVID LINN**
Art Director: David Linn
Client: AIGA San Francisco

▲ 514 **BARBARA HARTWELL**
Art Director: Robert Felsenstein
Client: CBS Records

▲ 515   **KINUKO Y. CRAFT**
Art Director: Alice Degenhardt
Client: Northwestern Mutual Life Insurance

◀ 516   **KINUKO Y. CRAFT**
Art Director: Alice Degenhardt
Client: Northwestern Mutual
                Life Insurance

▲ 517 **CONNIE CONNALLY**
Art Director: Kathy Rennels
Agency: Fahlgren & Swink
Client: Owens Illinois Forest Products Company

▶ 518 **RAY-MEL CORNELIUS**
Art Directors: Marcellina Kampa / David
Kampa
Client: Monarch Paper

▲ 519   **TOM KASPERSKI**
Art Director: Dave King

◀ 520   **MONTE DOLACK**

▲ 521   BRENT WATKINSON

▲ 522   BRENT WATKINSON   ▲ 523   BRENT WATKINSON

▲ 524   C. MICHAEL DUDASH

▲ 525 **JOEL SPECTOR**
Art Director: Leslie Rosenberg
Client: Oxford Industries

▶ 526 **MURRAY TINKLEMAN**
Art Director: Murray Tinkelman
Client: Harcourt, Brace, Jovanovich

◀ 527   D. M. DAVIDSON

▶ 529 **BILL NELSON**
Art Director: Bill Nelson
Client: Henrico County Public Schools

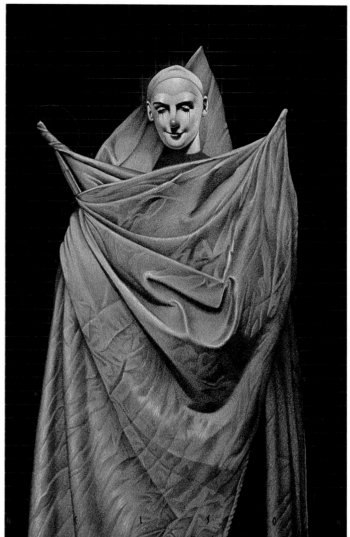

▲ 528 DEBORAH L. CHABRIAN

▶ 530 **LINDA HELTON**
Art Director: Ron Sullivan
Agency: Sullivan Perkins
Client: Rouse Company/South Street
Seaport

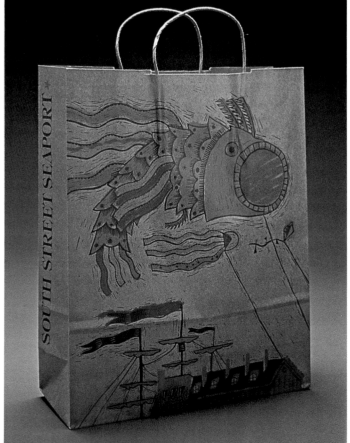

▲ 531   **BERNIE FUCHS**   ▼ 532   **DAVID LA FLEUR**
Art Director: Jack O'Grady
Agency: O'Grady Advertising Arts
Client: O'Grady Advertising Arts

Two Special Awards for 1988

The Society of Illustrators honors two men.

Dean Cornwell Achievement Award to Arthur Weithas For his leadership in expanding the Society as the center for illustration.

Arthur Weithas is a quiet man of strong conviction and fierce loyalty. His leadership and creative innovation have been evident throughout his distinguished career as art director, designer and fine artist. During World War II he received the Legion of Merit for his contributions as Art Director/Artist Correspondent of *Yank* magazine.

Arthur's commitment to the importance of illustration as an artistic and cultural medium was never more evident than when he co-chaired the stunning "200 Years of American Illustration" exhibition at the New-York Historical Society in 1976. Maintaining the theme, he created and chaired the "20 Years of Award Winners" exhibition; the book was also of his design.

Over the years the mark of his unerring taste and elegant style have been reflected in the historically important exhibitions which were his brain children: "America's Great Women Illustrators: 1850–1950," "The American Beauty," "René Bouché," "Eric," and the "Hall of Fame."

His design judgement is reflected in many special projects including the first Annual Student Scholarship Catalog and the "Art of Medicine" poster, as well as the book, *The Illustrator in America 1880–1980.* He was also editor of *Illustrators 24, 25, 26, 30.*

The importance of the Society's Museum of American Illustration cannot be overstated and as its first Director, Arthur's knowledge and appreciation was an inspiration. As Executive Vice President, Vice President, Co-Chairman of the Permanent Collection Committee and as a member of the Publications Committee, he excelled. We proudly reward Arthur for his commitment.

John Witt, Past President

*The Dean Cornwell Achievement Award
Arthur Weithas*

*The Arthur William Brown Recognition Award
Stevan Dohanos*

Arthur William Brown Recognition Award to Stevan Dohanos For his leadership in expanding the recognition of the importance of the illustrator.

When the word *Achievement* is used still again in conjunction with Steve Dohanos' name the question quickly occurs: what *Hasn't* he achieved?

If medals were awarded for past honors he'd stagger like a Russian General under the weight.

First, or course, came the overall recognition of his role in advertising and cover art over more than three decades.

At the height of this came his inclusion as one of the 10 original faculty members of the Famous Artists School.

Then came 3 selfless terms as President of the Society.

Meantime he was voted into our coveted Hall of Fame.

And then he became Design head of the U.S. Stamp program. It was during this time that many members came to know and appreciate him in a more personal way.

Next came an honor he cherishes: Honorary President; few have been so dubbed.

Recently the New Britain Museum of American Art, which has long benefited from his interest and efforts, staged a lifetime retrospective of his easel paintings.

That's one side of the coin: the Artist.

The flip side reveals the Good Citizen—and on all levels. He's not yet been heard to say *No* to requests for anything from church fairs to National drives. Mayors, Governors and a couple of U.S. Presidents have said "Thank You" to him. So do we.

It's a pleasure to raise our voices one more time to this unique man who has contributed so much—and there's plenty more where that came from.

Howard Munce

The Society of Illustrators

In 1901, the Society of Illustrators was founded "to promote and stimulate interest in the art of illustration, past, present and future." The early members included some of the major figures in American art: Charles Dana Gibson, N.C. Wyeth, Howard Pyle and William Glackens.

During World War I, enlistment posters were produced for the war effort including the famous James Montgomery Flagg "I Want You" portrait of Uncle Sam and the Charles Dana Gibson "I Wish I Were a Man" poster. Harvey Dunn and Wallace Morgan produced some of the great art reportage of the war.

Artist correspondents from the Society recorded WWII, the Korean conflict and the Vietnam War. The Society continues its contact with the services by providing voluntary illustrations for the Air Force and Coast Guard collections.

Throughout its history, the Society has always been deeply committed to educational programs and student scholarships.
The present program provides annual awards to college-level students, lectures for students and professionals and traveling exhibitions.

The Bicentennial Exhibition at the New-York Historical Society in 1976, "200 Years of American Illustration," revived and renewed interest in illustration not only as an art form but as a glowing record of American history and the mores of its people. Over 950 pieces of art were presented to record-breaking audiences. The exhibition and subsequent book were instrumental in reestablishing illustration at a time when it was challenged by photography and T.V. Bob Crozier was the Chairman, Art Weithas, Co-Chairman.

Illustration: Don Munson

The Museum

In February 1981, the 80th Anniversary of the founding of the Society, an extensive remodeling and expansion program was begun during the administration of John Witt. Made possible by contributions from members and generous support from J. Walter Thompson Company, two galleries were created and named The Museum of American Illustration. The expanded exhibition areas provided a showplace for exhibitions of not only the best of contemporary illustration through the Society's annual shows, but also theme

Members of the Museum Committee: l to r: Walt Reed; Wendell Minor; Dennis Kendrick; Art Weithas, Chairman; Diane Dillon; Howard Munce. Not present: Vincent DiFate, Tim Raglin, Bill Purdom, John Witt. Photo by Frank O'Blak.

exhibitions of ever-broadening interest to the public, i.e., the recent National Geographic Exhibition "The Artist Explores Our World," Science Fiction, Humor, Great American Women Illustrators, The New Illustration, The Art of Medicine, Dimensional Illustration, etc. One-man shows of the great illustrators, both past and contemporary, are also presented.

An expanded and refurbished library now provides an increasingly valuable source of information to researchers seeking biographical, manuscript and general memorabilia.

All the Society's projects function with the volunteer help of its dedicated members, devoted to the Society's original credo "to promote and stimulate interest in the art of illustration, past, present and future."

Arthur Weithas
Chairman, Museum Committee

National Geographic

One of the outstanding exhibitions of the year was "The Artist Explores Our World" celebrating the first hundred years of The National Geographic Society. Displayed were 171 works by 60 artists. Many members of the Society were represented in the show. It received excellent reviews and enjoyed excellent attendance.

The Society of Illustrators is appreciative that it was given the opportunity to first present this wonderful exhibition in its museum galleries.

The Artist Explores Our World

Society of Illustrators
Museum of American Illustrators

Readers often ask me how we get those wonderful photographs, and what settings do we use? My answer: f8 and *be* there! Those great images are made by getting up before dawn, by wrestling equipment to inaccessible places, by patiently waiting for the wildlife to return. And, often, they're made by shooting as if by instinct, or reflex, as an angry crowd closes in, and in some small way the world is forever changed.

But often a subject cannot be photographed, and that's when we turn to the incredible skills of the illustrator. He or she helps us see the past, and envision the future; shows us the insides of things that don't open, and captures the complex dynamics of how things work—how cells grow, how glaciers move.

This exhibition of 171 works by sixty artists is a sampling of the thousands of paintings and drawings National Geographic Society has commissioned in this century. Each piece, the work of a uniquely talented artist, is also the product of careful research and guidance by one of our dedicated art directors—Jan Adkins, Bob Teringo, Allen Carroll, Dave Seager, Jody Bolt, Vivi Silverman, Senior Assistant Editor Howard Paine, and, by the very able and long-time Art Editor, Andrew Poggenpohl.

This exhibition, and the catalog, is the work of National Geographic's art staff, working closely with Conservator Robin Siegel. Her enthusiasm, boundless energy, and hard work have produced a vibrant, exciting show.

The guiding spirit behind the Society's award-winning and trend-setting illustrations for the past three decades has been the brilliantly creative Art Director Howard E. Paine. He orchestrates the work of many talented contributors—and helps each bring something unique to the magazine. Each helps the reader understand, just a bit better, this complex, ever-changing world.

To the artists represented here I give hearty thanks, and a warning: watch out for the next century!

W.E. Garrett
Editor, National Geographic

△Noel Sickels
"Atocha Loads Up In Havana"

△Roy Andersen
"Pandora Shipwreck"

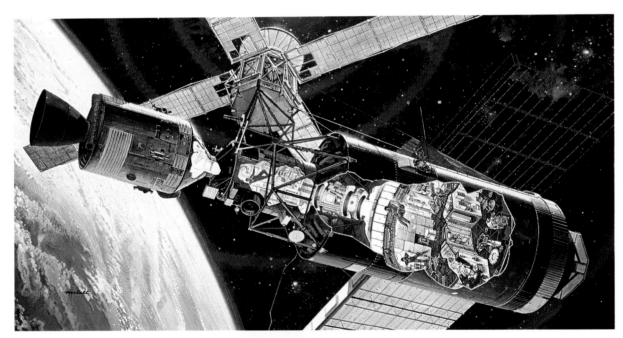

△Robert T. McCall
"Skylab"

◁Birney Lettick
"Byrd Antarctic Flight"

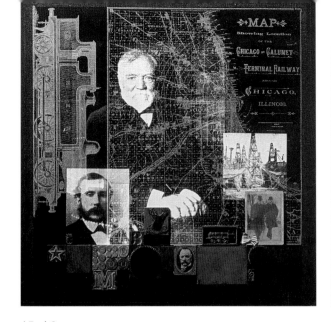

△Fred Otnes
"America In 1888, Industry"

△Morton
"Künstler·Port of Seleucia"

▽Peter Helck
"Citroen Haardt"

▽Paul Calle
"Sharks"

△Ken Dallison
"Flight of the Columbia"

◁Stanley Meltzoff
"John Harrison's Chronometer"

△N.C. Wyeth
"Duel On The Beach"

▽John Berkey
"Mary Rowlandson's Ordeal"

△Louis S. Glanszman
"Sam Adams & The Liberty Tree"

◁Kinuko Y. Craft
"Hagi"

Humor

Pretty damn dignified, all these Society exhibitions: eminently eminent Hall of Famers like René Bouché I mean how tasteful can you get? And how about 100 oh-so-reverent years of the National Geographic Society? Excuse me while I polish my pearls…

In an effort to create a balance between the sacred and profane, the Society held the 2nd Annual Humor Exhibition, Humor '88. In a nation-wide competition, entries of various persuasions were judged by the usual roundup of suspects: illustrators, art directors, cartoon editors. This hilarious group chose nearly 300 gags, single illustrations, political cartoons, and caricatures; awarded eleven Gold and Silver Funny Bones; and elected Charles Addams and George Herriman into the Humor Hall of Fame.

Irreverence, satire, outright lewdness were represented, as well as banana peel, plain funny. Great stuff, a terrific opening—enough to take the starch out of ol' Chuck Gibson's wing collar.

Jill Bossert
Exhibition Coordinator

Lou Myers
The Art Directors Club of New York

Arnold Roth
"Addicted to Love"
West

Steve Brodner
"Sam & Jerry Evening"
The Washington Post Magazine

Everett Peck
Paper Moon Graphics

Jill Wright
"Basis for a Lasting Relationship"
Recycled Paper Products

Mark A. Fredrickson
Anheuser Busch

Everett Peck
"Haute Pizza"
Playboy

Hall of Fame

The Hall of Fame Exhibition coincided with the Annual President's Dinner and the year's presentation of awards to the new inductees into the Hall of Fame and the Hamilton King winner.

It was a fitting occasion for this, the 30th Annual Hall of Fame celebration.

Representative paintings by all sixty recipients, both past and present, were on display in the museum galleries. It was an exhibition extraordinary for its quality and diversity. These pages offer a partial presentation of the Hall of Famers 1940–1988

Tom Lovell (b. 1909)
"Battle of Hastings"

Harold Von Schmidt (1893–1982)
"Horse Race"

Stevan Dohanos (b. 1907)
"The Coal Men"

Noel Sickels (1911–1982)
"Remains of the Prize" and "The Marlin Breaks Water"

Al Parker (1906–1985)
"Palm Court—Plaza Hotel"

Ben Stahl (1910–1987)
"She Turned a Wilderness into Home"

Coby Whitmore (1913–1988)
"Love is a Bargain"

Austin Briggs (1909–1973)
"General Omar Bradley, Viet Nam"

Haddon Sundblom (1899–1976)
"Never Say Die"

Albert Dorne (1904–1965)
"The Intruding Moose"

Jon Whitcomb (1906–1988)
"Brown–haired Gal"

Stan Galli (b. 1912)
"Blue Heron"

John Clymer (b. 1907)
"Schenck–Warlick Cotton Factory
near Lincolnton, North Carolina"

Bernie Fuchs (b. 1932)
"The Walking Circle"

Mark English (b. 1933)
"Repose"

Bob Peak (b. 1928)
"Missouri Breaks"

Robert Weaver (b. 1924)
"Plate Glass"

Ray Prohaska (1901–1981)
"Girl in Grass"

Al Hirschfeld (b. 1903)
"Zero Mostel"

James Montgomery Flagg (1877–1960)

Hall of Fame 1980

WWI recruiting poster
Collection: Ed Verball

Four decades enjoyed his illustrations, during which time he produced a staggering amount of work. Monty estimated he produced a drawing a day, or over 300 pictures a year. And he also found time to write articles and books, movie scenarios and plays. He did sculpture, painted in oils.

And his work needed no signature.

Everything he did was uniquely Flagg; his manner of speaking, his eyebrows. He himself had, as he said of his great crony Jack Barrymore, "as many brilliant facets as a fly's eye."

Regardless of medium, everything he touched was marked by taste, style and vitality. For Monty, all art was feeling, and the medium merely the means to express it.

"Monty" Flagg despised sham, he loved beauty: men, women, or children, landscapes, anything, anywhere, anytime. If you pinned him down, he'd admit his favorite form of beauty was woman. And he loved laughter!

Everett Raymond Kinstler

"The Protective Instinct"

Annual Scholarship Competition

The Annual Student Competition was another successful venture with 4,300 entries, 124 selected, and a total of $30,000 given away to the award-winning youngsters. Hallmark increased their generous contribution to $30,000 this year and I'd like to thank all those companies and individuals who so graciously support this important area of the Society.

The awards presentation went very well with 28 of the 32 award-winning students attending from all around the country.

Along with this annual competition, we have the Charles Dana Gibson Memorial Scholarship, a full tuition, fees and materials grant. Eun Ju Kang from Art Center College of Design in Pasadena proved to be a very worthy first recipient, and it's interesting to note that she was also the top award winner in our Annual Student Competition this year. (Her piece was selected without anyone knowing who did the work.)

Chang Park, our second Gibson Scholar (also from Art Center), arrived in New York in time for his review and proved to be another very worthy recipient.

The entries for the Al Dorne Scholarship, a tuition award for talented and needy students in the five boroughs, were reviewed in June. Dennis Murphy (FIT) and Drew Bishop (SVA) received awards this year. This scholarship program is chaired by Jacques Parker.

I'd also like to thank all of the jurors who graciously gave of their time and effort, Beverly Sacks who successfully runs our Christmas auction, and Peter Fiore for his support and efforts.

You surely know how grateful these students are, and how much these awards mean to them...the illustrators of tomorrow.

Eileen Hedy Schultz
Chairman, Scholarship Committee

Eun Ju Kang with her award-winning illustration.

Society Members Salute Pratt Institute's 100th Anniversary

Many an artist points with pride to the guiding hand of an important art teacher. For the last 100 years, Pratt Institute has supplied that guiding hand, and the recipients of that institution have formed a cadre of America's leading influential artists.

The Society of Illustrators points with pride to the many members who have called Pratt Institute their alma mater since the Society's founding in 1901. We were therefore pleased to present this group show of our current Members/Pratt graduates.

The excellence of these established artists affirms Pratt's ongo-ing academic prominence. The vitality and expressiveness of the younger professionals' works show Pratt's openness and dynamic approach to changing art styles.

The Society of Illustrators and Pratt Institute have each had a long and storied history. This group show—Society Members Salute Pratt Institute's 100th Anniversary—was a pleasant pause along the way.

Diane Dillon
President, Society of Illustrators

First art illustration class, 1887, Pratt Institute Archives

MEMBERS OF SOCIETY OF ILLUSTRATORS WHO STUDIED AT PRATT INSTITUTE

Ruth Bugzester, '45	Dwight Dobbins, '57	Mort Kunstler, '50	Donald Moss, '49	Mariam Schottland, '57
Paul Calle, '47	Elaine Duillo, '49	Roy LaGrone, '49	Howard Munce, '38	Art Seiden, '40
Tony Capone, '48	Naiad Einsel, '47	Richard Lebenson, '66, '68	Malcolm Murley, '34	Ned Seidler
Marilyn Church, '59	Peter Fiore	Forbes Linkhorn, '57	Barbara Nessim, '60	Arthur Shilstone, '47
Art Cumings, '47	Al Fortunato, '49, '53	*Albert Lorenz, '65	Tom Nikosey, '72	Attilio Sinagra, '39
Bernard D'Andrea, '43	Eric Fowler, '78	Mike Machat	Julia Noonan, '68	Milda Vizbar, '68
Diane De Groat, '69	Michael Garland, '74	Jeffrey Mangiat, '75	Heide Oberheide, '79	Randi Wasserman, '68
	Robert George, '73	Richard Mantel, '63	Alvin Pimsler, '38	George Wilson, '47
	Salvatore Giglio, '52	Frank Mayo, '68	Al Pisano	
	Glenn Harrington, '81	Charles J. Mazoujian, '39	Barnett Plotkin, '52	
	George Kelvin, '51	James McMullan, '58	Harry Rosenbaum	*Graduated School of
	Howard Koslow, '44	Jacqui Morgan, '60	Barry Ross, '59	Architecture

The Dimensional Illustrator

After 87 years of Society exhibitions that have consisted mostly of images rendered on canvas, gessoed panels or Whatman Board and made to lay flat against our gallery walls, "The Dimensional Illustrator" show broke the mold. It intruded *into* the room!

Thirty-seven members fashioned and wrought 70 dimensional works made from everything from baked dough to welded steel. Most objects either stood from the walls, dangled from them or cast shadows upon them. Our Founders could be heard whirling in distant graves.

The show was theatrical, clever, skillful, provocative and exciting.

It showed the illustrator released from illusion, producing in the round. When the lights came up at the opening reception and revealed the great variety of gleaming objects all in unplanned juxtaposition, with their great variety of materials, colors, textures and conceptions, it became a razzle-dazzle room to behold. And it was contagious: the gallery party buzzed...almost in three dimensions!

Howard Munce
Exhibition Chairman

Photo: Jim Herity/Design: Howard Munce

Government Services

The Society continued its participation in both the U.S. Air Force Art Program and U.S. Coast Guard Illustration Program during our 1987–1988 year. Under both programs, Society artists are invited to participate on merit, demonstrated interest, style, and skills appropriate for the particular mission to be documented.

The Air Force furnishes reimbursement for costs and transportation and pays a per diem to cover expenses, while the Coast Guard provides an honorarium to cover these costs. The artist donates his or her time, original art and the right to reproduce the work for government purposes only. The artist retains the copyright in the work if he or she wishes.

Budgetary considerations have reduced the opportunities for members participating in our Air Force program, but we have had some most interesting trips. We thank those who have participated during the past year and are particularly pleased to include members who have been involved for the first time.

Keith Ferris
Chairman, Government Services Committee

Dean Ellis
"U.S. Coast Guard Intercept of Soviet Surveillance Ship, Montauk Point," 1986

Gil Cohen
"M A C Security Police," 1987

Shannon Stirnweis

From Wild Life to the Wild West to Wild Lovers, Shannon Stirnweis' art has encompassed a diversity of subjects to challenge the most versatile of talents. Yet, he engages each category with great gusto and carries us along with his authority.

Whether commissioned by a commercial client or painted for a gallery exhibit, Shannon has taken on each picture as a fresh experience and made it exciting to share with him.

Walt Reed

"The Challanger"
Field & Stream

Shannon Stirnweis is represented in the Department of Interior, U.S. Air Force Historical Collection, Allstate, CBS, U.S. Army Historical Museum, Burt Reynolds, Marriott, Leaning Tree, Grumbacher, U.S. Air Force Academy, University of Wyoming and California Federal Savings Collections. He was President of the Society of Illustrators 1972–74 and a Founding Trustee of the Graphic Artists Guild in New York.

Douglas Gorsline (1913–1985)

Douglas Gorsline had the unique ability to shift smoothly from his own private art into the art of illustration. He brought the same high standards and integrity to his commissioned assignments that he gave to his personal artistic expression.

Douglas enjoyed the role of the artist-reporter. He loved to travel to the scene of sporting events, mingling with the crowd and the players. He brought to these sports portfolios his gifts of the superb draftsman and the keen observer. His finished paintings were accomplished through his private vision which reminded me of some strange inner lens that only he could call upon.

Richard Gangel
Art Director, Sports Illustrated 1960–1981

"The Last Bareknuckle Fight"
Sports Illustrated, 1977

John Holmgren (1897–1963)

Holmgren joined the Society of Illustrators as soon after his arrival in New York as he was eligible. When the Society outgrew its East 23rd Street quarters, (and had some cash in the bank because the Shuberts had bought the rights to an Illustrators' "Artists and Models" show for Broadway) Holmgren was among those appointed to LeRoy "Sport" Ward's committee to find new space. In 1939 the building they located on East 63rd Street became the Society's permanent home.

From 1941 to 1944 Johnny was the Society's President. Among the projects he spearheaded was the volunteer program to sketch the hospitalized war wounded, and the "Loose Talk Can Cost Lives" poster series for the British and American Ambulances Services. Active on many Society fronts, Holmgren particularly enjoyed the role of "extra" and/or scenery painter for the annual show. He was elected a Life Member and his final service to the Society was as manager of the Relief Fund.

Frances Holmgren Costikyan

"What Do You Know?"
Collection: Society of Illustrators
Museum of American Illustration

Members

The Members' Gallery is the exhibit space opposite the bar on the third floor of the Society's building—just at the entrance to the dining room. It is for members and is a popular place for showing recent or experimental work.

Mitchell Hooks
Members Exhibition Chairman

Anita Marci

John Burgoyne

Don Munson

Steve Brodner

David Grove

New Acquisitions

Leo and Diane Dillon
"San Diego Lightfoot Sue"
Donated by the Artists

O ver the past three years more than 250 pieces have been donated by nearly 100 donors, representing the work of approximately 200 artists, most of whom have not appeared in the Collection before. We wish to extend our thanks to the J. Walter Thompson Company and to American Cyanamid for their generosity and support over many years. Our special thanks go also to the many contemporary artists who have understood the needs of the Collection, realized the importance of its mission and given their finest works to insure its future.

Vincent Di Fate
Chairman, Permanent Collection

Jack Davis
"Caveman"
Donated by Elaine Duillo

Brad Holland
"Eye to Eye with Mr. T"
Donated by the Artist

Mitchell Hooks
"Woman in Front of Movie Theatre"
Donated by the Artist

Madison Square Press: Jill Bossert, Delia Doherty, Arpi Ermoyan, Roberto Glinoga, Zulema Rodriguez, Kathy Spadoni

deCesare Design Associates: Connie Huebner, Sandra Collette, Kathy Cotaling, Sean Garretson, Katie Marchese

Cover, details of illustrations by (top row) John Hom, Blair Drawson, Paul Davis, (bottom row) Richard Mantel, Thomas Blackshear II, and Guy Billout

Typographer: Arnold and Debel Inc.

Photo Credits: Hall of Fame/Bob McCall by Robert Schulman—NASA; Award Winners/Blair Drawson by Michael Rafelson; John Craig by Carolyn Potts; Elwood H. Smith by Andrew Wainwright. Jurors/Walt Spitzmiller by Maureen Fennelli; Miriam Schottland by Donald Perry; Mary Zisk by Tim O'Conner. Dean Cornwell Recognition Award/Art Weithas, Arthur William Brown Recognition Award/Stevan Dohanos and Charles Dana Gibson Memorial Scholarship/Eun Ju Kang by George Kanatous.

Tom Wolfe introduction Copyright © 1978 by The New York Times Company. Reprinted by permission

HALL OF FAME GATEFOLD:

Frederic Sackrider Remington
Amon Carter Museum of Western Art

Charles Dana Gibson
Society of Illustrators Museum of American Illustration (SIMAI)

Edwin Austin Abbey
On loan from the Yale University Art Gallery to the SIMAI

J.C. Leyendecker
The Saturday Evening Post cover, 1934
SIMAI

Winslow Homer
The Butler Institute of American Art

Harvey T. Dunn
SIMAI

N.C. Wyeth
SIMAI

Howard Chandler Christy
Illustration House, Inc.

Frederic R. Gruger
SIMAI

Norman Rockwell
The Saturday Evening Post
SIMAI

Henry Patrick Raleigh
Maxwell House Coffee
Mr. & Mrs. Elliot Liskin Purchase Fund SIMAI

Wallace Morgan
Stars and Stripes, 1918

Dean Cornwell
J. Walter Thompson Company
Purchase Fund SIMAI

Walter Biggs
SIMAI

Floyd MacMillan Davis
Eleanor Martin Cory Estate Purchase Fund SIMAI

Saul Tepper
Redbook, 1934
SIMAI

Carl Erickson
Vogue cover, 1936
Collection of Janet and Arthur Weithas

Robert Fawcett
SIMAI

Rockwell Kent
From *Moby Dick*
J. Walter Thompson Company
Purchase Fund SIMAI

Neysa Moran McMein
McCall's cover
Illustration House, Inc.

John LaGatta
SIMAI

HALL OF FAME 1940–1988

Tom Lovell
National Geographic Society

Harold Von Schmidt
Esquire, 1950
SIMAI

Stevan Dohanos
The Saturday Evening Post cover
SIMAI

Noel Sickles
Life, 1952
SIMAI

Ben Stahl
John Hancock Life Insurance
SIMAI

Al Parker
American Airlines, 1950s
J. Walter Thompson Company
Purchase Fund SIMAI

Austin Briggs
On permanent loan from Tom Holloway

Coby Whitmore
The Ladies' Home Journal, 1947
J. Walter Thompson Company
Purchase Fund SIMAI

Haddon Sundblom
The Ladies' Home Journal, 1938
SIMAI

Albert Dorne
The Saturday Evening Post
SIMAI

Jon Whitcomb
Society of Illustrators Members
Purchase Fund

Stan Galli
On loan from Weyerhauser Paper Company

Bernie Fuchs
The Franklin Library
Anonymous donation

John Clymer
American Cyanamid
SIMAI

Bob Peak
Courtesy of artist

Mark English
Courtesy of artist

Robert Weaver
Audience Magazine
Courtesy of artist

Ray Prohaska
McCall's
SIMAI

Al Hirschfeld
Margot Feiden Galleries

CLIENTS

MAGAZINES, PUBLISHERS, AND PUBLICATIONS

AGENCIES

Abbett, Robert
Abel, Raymond
Abrams, Kathie
Accornero, Franco
Acuna, Ed
Adams, Jeanette
Adler, Kermit
Adorney, Charles
Albright, Nina
Alexander, Hugh B.
Alexander, Paul
Allen, Betty H.
Allen, Patricia J.
Altekruse, Max
Ambler, Louise
Ammirati, Carlo
Anderson, Lyman
Anderson, Richard
Anthony, Al
Anthony, Robert
Appleby, Ellen H.
Arevalo, Walter
Arisman, Marshall
Armstrong, Susan
Aronson, Mrs. Alice
Asciutto, Mary Anne
Auth, Tony
Bacon, Paul
Bald, Ken
Barban, John A.
Barberis, Juan C.
Barkley, James
Barlowe, Wayne
Barron, Don
Barry, James E.
Bauer, Geri
Beall, Jr., Lester
Beck, David M.
Bender, Gerald D.
Bennett, Brad
Benney, Robert
Benton, Jr., Harrison E.
Berd, Elliot
Berenson, Richard
Berger, Charles J.
Berkey, John C.
Berkley, Sy
Berman, Craig
Bernstein, Samuel
Berran, Robert
Berry, Park
Berte, June Allard
Bertolami, Peter J.
Billout, Guy
Birmingham, Lloyd P.
Bjorklund, Charles R.
Blattner, Robert H.
Blickenstaff, Wayne K.
Bliok, Leo
Bode, Robert
Boies, Alexandra
Bolger, William F.
Bomar, Mrs. Walter
Bonavita, Donna M.
Bond, Higgins
Bonvino, Michael
Booth, George W.
Botscheller, Mimi
Bouffard, John J.
Bowie, Effie
Bowler, Jr., Joseph
Boyd, Douglas
Brackett, Ward
Bralds, Braldt
Bramwell, Randolph
Brandon, Elinore

Brauer, Fred J.
Brennan, Ed
Bridges, Victor
Brindle, Melbourne
Brinkman, John H.
Brison-Stack, Guy
Brodner, Steve
Brooks, Andrea
Brooks, Joe
Brooks, Lou
Brooks, Mrs. Lois
Brown, Craig MacFarlan
Brown, Daniel J.
Brown, Marbury Hill
Brown, Michael David
Brown, Peter A.
Buchanan, Yvonne
Buck, Barbara
Bugzester, Ruth
Burgoyne, John
Burns, Charles
Busch, Mrs. Shelley
Butcher, Lawrence
Cagle, Daryl
Calle, Paul
Calman, Mel
Campbell, Stuart
Canniff, Bryan
Capobianco, Michael R.
Capone, Anthony J.
Caporale, Wende
Carr, Barbara
Carr, Charles Noell
Carter, Charles Henry
Catalano, Al
Cavanagh, Tom
Cellini, Joseph
Chaite, Alexander E.
Channell, John W.
Charles, Milton
Charmatz, Bill
Chaykin, Howard
Church, Marilyn
Ciardiello, Joseph
Clarke, Grace D.
Clarke, James V.
Clarke, Mrs. Rene
Clemente, Thomas Frank
Clifford, Judy Dean
Clinton, Brian
Closi, Victor J.
Cober, Alan E.
Coconis, Ted
Cohen, Gil
Combs, Robert Mason
Conge, Bob
Conley, John J.
Conlon, William J.
Connell, Hugh
Connolly, Howard
Connolly, Joseph
Consor, James Bowman
Content, Dan
Cooper, Mario
Copeland, Arnold J.
Cornell, Jeffrey W.
Corvington, Mark
Cosgrove, Jerry L.
Counihan, Gerald T.
Cox, Peter
Cox, Robert
Craft, Kinuko
Cramer, PhD, D. L.
Crawford, Emma
Crawford, Robert
Crawford, Tad

Crofut, Bob
Crouse, Danny
Crowell, James
Crowley, Donald V.
Crozier, Bob
Csatari, Joseph
Cuevas, Robert J.
Cumings, Arthur
Cunningham, Robert M.
Cusano, Steven R.
D'Andrea, Bernard
D'Antin, E. Alba Teran
Dacey, Bob
Daily, Don
d'Alessio, Gregory
Dallison, Ken
Daly, Tom
Darling, Lois
Davidian, Anna
Davidson, Dennis M.
Davidson, Everett
Davies, Ken
Davis, Bill
Davis, Bob A.
Davis, Jack
Davis, Joseph
Davis, Marshall
Davis, Omar G.
Davis, Paul
Davisson, Mrs. Zita
deCesare, John
Declercq, Gilbert
Degenhardt, Alice L.
DeGroat, Diane
Della-Piana, Elissa
Del Rey, Lester
Demarest, Robert J.
DeMers, Janice
Deneen, James Bennett
Deschamps, Robert
Descombes, Roland J.
Deverin, Daniele
Devlin, Harry
Di Gianni, John
Dicicco, Gilbert E.
Dickerson, James
DiFate, Vincent
Dillon, Diane
Dillon, Leo
Dittrich, Dennis
Dobbins, Dwight
Dohanos, Stevan
Dolwick, William A.
Donner, Carol
Doolittle, Melanie
Drendel, Lou
Dubowski, Donald E.
Duffy, William R.
Duillo, Elaine
Dula, William
Dumm, Edwina
Dyekman, James E.
Dystel, Oscar
Eagle, Eugene
Early, Mrs. Walter
Echevarria, Abe
Effron, Barbara
Egan, Jr., Albert F.
Egner, Thomas
Ehrhardt, Eleanor
Einsel, Naiad
Einsel, Walter
Eisenberg, Monroe
Eisman, Arthur
El Masri, Hani
Ellis, Dean

Ellis, Jonathan
Elton, Wallace W.
Emmett, Bruce
Endewelt, Jack
English, Mark
Ennis, John
Enokido, Fumihiko
Epstein, Lorraine Mosely
Erikson, Rolf
Erlacher, Bill
Ermoyan, Arpi
Ermoyan, Suren
Evans, Nancy
Falcone, Allen C.
Falk, Gustave
Falls, Mrs. C. B.
Farnsworth, Bill
Feagans, Jr., Thomas I.
Federico, Helen
Feinen, Jeffrey F.
Fennimore, Linda
Ferguson, M. Carr
Ferris, Keith
Fetzer, Craig
Filippucci, Sandra
Finch, Jr., Mrs. Ralph
Fiore, Peter M.
Fisher, Gordon
Fisher, Leonard E.
Fitzgerald, John E.
Flanagan, John
Fletcher, William
Flory, Verdon
Folkman, Janice
Forbes, Bart J.
Foreman, Robert
Fortunato, Al
Fortunato, Carol
Forzaglia, John J.
Fowler, Eric
Francis, Judy
Frankfurt, Stephen O.
Fraser, Betty
Frater, Hal
Frazer, William L.
Freitag, Samuel
Frith, Michael K.
Froom, Georgia
Fuchs, Bernard
Fujikawa, Gyo
Fujita, Makoto
Gaadt, George S.
Gallagher, James
Galli, Stanley W.
Gallo, Bill
Gamache, John
Garland, Michael
Garn, (Duenwald) Doris
Gaydos, John
Gayler, Anne
Gehm, Charles C.
Genova, Joseph
George, Robert J.
Germakian, Michael
Gersten, Gerry
Giglio, Salvatore
Gildar, Carol
Ginsburg, Max
Giordano, Richard
Girard, Samuel
Gist, Linda
Gittelson, Anders
Giusti, Bob
Glanzman, Louis S.
Glass, Charles
Glattauer, Ned

Gleason, Paul M.
Glick, Judith
Glissmeyer, Garry W.
Gold, Bill
Goldberg, Mrs. Rube
Golton, Glen
Gordon, Barbara
Gossett, Milton
Goudeau, Cleven
Graber, Norman
Graham, Mariah
Gramatky, Mrs. Hardie
Grant, A. Leigh
Grau, Julie
Gray, George
Greene, Darrel
Greene, Joshua M.
Greenhalgh, Robert F.
Greenwald, Herbert
Gregori, Leon
Grider, Dick
Grien, Anita
Gromoll, Kim
Grote, Richard
Grothkopf, Chad M.
Grove, David
Gruppo, Nelson
Guggenheimer, Charles S.
Guzzi, George
Guzzi, Mrs. Rita M.
Haber, Zelda
Hafner, Marylin
Hall, Bruce W.
Hall, Deborah Ann
Hall, H. Tom
Hallock, Mrs. Robert
Hama, Sho-Ichiro
Hamilton, Edward
Hamilton, Richard
Hampton, Blake
Hamrick, Chuck
Handler, Murray R.
Handville, Robert T.
Hankins, David
Hantman, Carl E.
Hardaway, Ronald H.
Hardy, Neil
Harrington, Glenn
Harris, James R.
Harris, Robert G.
Hart, Veronica
Harte, Cheryl A.
Hartman, Bill
Hashimoto, Hirokazu
Hatton, Enid Vaune
Hawes, Charles M.
Hawkey, William Steven
Healy, Deborah
Hedin, Donald M.
Heimann, Steven
Heindel, Robert
Hejja, Attila
Helck, Mrs. Peter
Heller, Ruth
Helzer, James A.
Henderson, David F.
Herald, Robert S.
Herbert, Mrs. James
Herrick, Ira
Hess, Mark
Hill, Sidney
Hines, Jack
Hinojosa, Albino R.
Hodges, Mrs. David
Hoffmann, Nancy L.
Hoffmann, Mrs. Ginnie

Hoie, Claus
Holland, Raymond E.
Holmgren, Mrs. John
Hooks, Mitchell
Hortens, Mrs. Margaret
Hosaka, Mitsutoshi
Hoskins, Frances
Hosner, William
Hotchkiss, Wesley G.
Huerta, Catherine
Huerta, Gerard
Hunt, Peter F.
Hunt, Robert
Hurst, Mrs. Earl O.
Huyssen, Roger
Ilic, Mirko
Ilsley, Velma
Ishmael, Woodi
Iskowitz, Joel
Jaffee, Allan
James, Bill
Jamison, John
Jankovitz, Frank
Jasper, (Tsao) Jacqueline
    Ann
Jensen, Enola G.
Johnson, Alfred
Johnson, Cecile
Johnson, Diane Elizabeth
Johnson, Don
Johnson, Doug
Johnson, Evelyne
Johnson, Gordon A.
Johnson, Lewis P.
Johnson, Max D.
Johnston, Don
Jones, George
Jones, Keith Robert
Jones, Robert
Jones, Taylor
Jonson, Jim
Jossel, Marguerite
Juhasz, Victor
Just, Hal
Kadin, Charles B.
Kahn, Harvey
Kalback, Jerry A.
Kamen, Jack
Karl, Gerald T.
Karlin, Bernard
Kastel, Roger
Katinas, Jr., Charles C.
Kaufman, Joe
Kelvin, George V.
Kemble, John
Kemper, Bud
Kendrick, Dennis
Kenny, Charlotte
Kent, Albert J.
Kessler, Leonard
Kidder, Harvey
Kimmelman, Phil
King, Jean Callan
King, Mrs. Joseph
King, Mrs. Warren
King, Stanley
Kinstler, Everett Raymond
Kirchoff, Morris A.
Kitts, Thomas J.
Klavins, Uldis
Klein, David
Klein, Donald
Klimt, Bill
Koenigsberg, Marvin
Kohler, Keith
Kohfield, Richard

Koslow, Howard
Kossin, Sanford
Kowalski, Raymond A.
Kramer, Dick
Kretschman, Karin
Kristoff, Jeri
Krush, Beth
Krush, Joseph P.
Kubista, John
Kurie, Elaine
Kurzweil, Hannah
Kuze, Akiko
Laager, Ken
Lacano, Frank
Lachowicz, Cheryl
Ladnier, Paul
LaGrone, Roy E.
Lamacchia, Frank
Lamarque, Abril
Lander, Jane
Lane, Leslie
Lapham, Mrs. Robert
LaPick, John
Lapsley, Robert
Larkin, David
LaRoche, LouAnne
Larson, Esther
Laukhuf, Lawrence A.
Lavin, Robert
Law, Polly M.
Lawrence, Lydia
Lazzaro, Victor A.
Lebenson, Richard A.
Lee, Bill
Lee, Jared
Lee, Nan Roberts
Lee, Robert J.
Lee, Tom
Lee, Warren E.
Leggett, Mrs. Barbara
Leifer, Martin
Leone, Leonard P.
Lesh, David
Lettick, Mrs. Birney
Levy, Frank
Lewin, Robert L.
Lieber, Larry
Light, Eugene
Lika, Arthur
Linkhorn, Forbes
Lisieski, Peter A.
Liskin, Mrs. Joyce
Lively, Alton L.
Livingston, Mrs. Robert C.
Llewellyn, Mrs. William
Locke, Nonnie
Lockwood, Mrs. Richard C.
Long, Charles A.
Longtemps, Kenneth
Loomis, Henry R.
Lopker, Gately Mrs.
    Virginia
Lorenz, Albert
Lott, George
Lovell, Tom
Lowry, Alfred
Lubey, Richard
Lucas, Robert O.
Luke, John H.
Lunde, Thomas
Lupo, Dom
Lustig, Loretta E.
Lutz, William J.
Luzak, Dennis
Lyall, Dennis
Lynch, Donald C.

Lyons, Ellen G.
Macaulay, Mary
MacDonald, John D.
MacFayden, Cornelia
Machat, Michael
Magagna, Anna Marie
Makris, Nancy L.
Maltese, Constance Mary
Mandel, Bette
Manger, Nina
Mangiat, Jeffrey
Manham, Allan
Maniere, James L.
Manning, Burton J.
Mantel, Richard
Marchetti, Louis J.
Marci, Anita
Marcus, Helen
Marden, Phil
Marmaras, John S.
Martignette, Jr., Charles G.
Marx, Marcia
Mason, Fred R.
Mathieu, Joe
Matsushita, Susumu
Mattelson, Marvin
Mattingly, David
Mawicke, Tran
Mayo, Frank
Mays, Maxwell
Mazoujian, Charles J.
McCaffery, Janet
McCall, Robert
McCollum, Rick
McConnell, Gerald
McDaniel, Jerry
McDermott, John R.
McDowell, Lynn Baynon
McEntire, Larry
McGinnis, Robert E.
McIntosh, Jon
McKeown, Gloria
McLean, Wilson
McMahon, Eileen
McMullan, James
McNeeley, Tom
McPheeters, Neal
McVicker, Charles
McWilliams, Clyde
Mee, William
Meglin, Nick
Meisel, Ann
Mendelsohn, Michael
Mendez, Toni
Mendola, Joe
Menk, France
Merrill, Abby
Meyer, Gary
Meyer, Jackie M.
Meyers, Newton
Milbourn, Pat
Miller, Claudia
Miller, Don
Miller, Phillip
Millington, John
Milne, Jonathan
Minor, Wendell
Minuto, Doreen
Miranda, Michael P.
Mistretta, Andrea
Mogel, Allan
Montebello, Joseph E.
Moodie, Mrs. Zandra
Morgan, Jacqui
Morgan, Vicki
Mori, Sadahito

Morrill, Jr., Richard D.
Morrison, William L.
Morrissey, Georgia
Moscarello, Robert A.
Moschetti, Frank J.
Moshier, Harry
Moss, Donald F.
Moss, Geoffrey
Moss, Tobias
Mott, Herb
Munce, Howard
Munson, Donald
Murley, Malcolm L.
Murphy, Harry
Murphy, John Cullen
Musler, Joel
Muth, Donald W.
Mutz, Marie
Myers, Lou
Nagaoka, Shusei
Najaka, Marlies Merk
Napoli, Augie
Nathan, Eunice
Neail, Pamela R.
Neale, Russell
Neglia, Josephine
Neher, Fred
Neill, Mrs. John R.
Nelson, Carey Boone
Nessim, Barbara
Netter, M.D., Frank H.
Newborn, Milton
Newman, Frederick R.
Newman, George
Newman, Susan
Nichol, Richard J.
Nikosey, Tom
Noonan, Julia
Norem, Earl H.
Noring, Soren
North, Russell C.
Notarile, Chris
Oberheide, Heide
Oksner, Robert M.
Olbinski, J. Rafal
Olivere, Raymond L.
Orioles, Agnes
Osonitsch, Robert
Osyczka, Bohdan D.
Otnes, Fred
Paces, Zlata
Packer, A. Shore
Paine, Howard
Palmer, Thomas J.
Palulian, Dickran
Parios, Arnold
Park, William B.
Parker, Ed
Parker, Jacques
Parker, Mrs. Al
Pasquini, Eric
Passen, Addie
Paugh, Tom
Payne, George
Peak, Bob
Pecoraro, Patricia
Pedersen, B. Martin
Pennor, Robert Russell
Pepper, Brenda
Pepper, Robert
Percivalle, Roseanne
Pereida, Ralph J.
Perrone, Angelo A.
Peters, Bob
Petro, Joseph V.
Philadelphia Art Institute

Phillips, Robert
Phipps, Alma
Picard, Thomas E.
Pimsler, Alvin J.
Pinkney, Jerry
Pisano, Alfred
Plotkin, Barnett
Polenberg, Myron
Popko, Stan
Popp, Walter
Porter, George
Portner, Richard
Portuesi, Louis
Pozefsky, Carol
Prato, Rodica
Pratt Institute Comm.
    Design Dep.
Prestopino, Robert
Price, Alice
Privitello, Michael
Prohaska, Mrs. Ray
Prusmack, Jon
Puder, Richard
Purdom, William S.
Putt, Glenna
Pyle, Willis A.
Queyroy, Anny
Quon, Mike
Rabut, Mrs. Paul
Radice, Judi
Raglin, Timothy C.
Rainer, Andrea
Ramsay
Ramus, Mike
Rapp, Gerald M.
Raymond, Frank
Reed, Robert D.
Reed, Roger
Reed, Walt
Reich, Heio W.
Renfro, Ed
Rey, Marilyn
Reynolds, Keith
Reynolds, Scott
Rhode Island School of
    Design
Richards, Irene D.
Richards, Walter D.
Ringling School of Design
Ritter, Arthur D.
Robbins, Lisa
Rockmore, Mrs. Julian A.
Roda II, John B. (BOT)
Rogers, Warren
Rogoff, Herbert
Roman, Helen
Romary, Jr., Alfred J.
Ronalds, Bill
Ronga, Wendy
Roseman, Mill
Rosenbaum, Harry
Rosier, Lydia
Ross, Barry
Ross, Don
Ross, Gordon
Ross, Ruth
Rossi, Joseph O.
Rossin, Lester
Roth, Arnold
Rothovius, Iska
Rowe, Charles
Rudd, Gregory
Rudenjak, Phyllis
Sacks, Beverly
Sacks, Cal
Sacks, Shelly

Safan, Elane Gutman
Sahni, Tiia Taks
Saks, Robert A.
Sanjulian, Manuel P.
Santore, Charles
Sass, Sidney
Sauber, Rob
Saylor, Steven S.
Schaare, Harry J.
Schallack, Mrs. Augie
Schleinkofer, David J.
Schmeck, Heidi L.
Schmelzer, John P.
Schneider, Mrs. Nellie
Schoenherr, John C.
School of Visual Arts
Schorr, Kathy S.
Schorr, Todd
Schottland, Miriam
Schreck, John
Schreiber, Dana
Schulman, Lowell M.
Schulman, Robert
Schultz, Eileen Hedy
Schulz, Mrs. Robert E.
Schwarz, Jill K.
Scianna, Cosimo
Scott, Mrs. John
Seaver, Jeff
Seiden, Art
Seidler, Ned M.
Selby, Robert
Semler, Robert C.
Shallis, Janice "Lynn"
Sharpe, James C.
Shaw, Barclay
Shaw, Wm. Theodore
Shealy, Mrs. George A.
Shearer, Julie E.
Shepardson, Betsy
Shepherd, Judith
Shilstone, Arthur
Shoemaker, Col. Alan
Shook, Mrs. Florence
Shore, Robert
Sidebotham, Jack
Siegel, Leo Dink
Silber, Maurice
Silverman, Robert
Simard, Claude
Simon, A. Christopher
Sinagra, Attilio
Sinovcic, Miro
Skypeck, George L.
Smith, Douglas B.
Smith, Gail Hunter
Smith, Marilyn A.
Smith, Paul R.
Smith, Robert S.
Smith, Stanley
Smith, Stephen
Smollin, Michael J.
Soileau, Hodges
Soldwedel, Kipp
Solie, John Andrew
Solomon, Richard
Soper, Pat
Sorel, Edward
Sowinski, Walter D.
Spanfeller, James
Spiak, Sharon
Spitzmiller, Walter A.
Spollen, Christopher J.
Stanton, Mindy Phelphs
Stasolla, Mario L.
Steadham, Richard

Steadman, Evan T.
Stech, Dave
Stein, Harve
Steinbrenner, Karl H.
Sterrett, Jane
Stewart, Arvis L.
Stillerman, Roberta
Stirnweis, Shannon
Stone, David K.
Stone, Sylvia
Storch, Otto
Stretton, Gertrude
Stromberg, Mike
Stroud, Steven H.
Stuart, Neil
Suh, Jeongin
Sullivan, Brian
Sullivan, Suzanne Hughes
Sumichrast, Józef
Swanson, Robert
Sweeney, Brian M.
Sweet, Robin
Taback, Simms
Takahashi, Kyo
Tanabe, Masakazu
Tanen, Norman
Tanenbaum, Robert
Tanner, Bert
Tardiff, Melissa
Tauchert, Herman
Tauss, Herbert
Tauss, Jack
Taylor, Dahl
Teaford, Lee
Teason, William I.
Tennant, Craig
Tennison, James
Tepper, Matthew
Teringo, J. Robert
Theryoung, Richard
Thompson, Eugene
Thompson, J. Bradbury
Thompson, John
Thompson, Kenneth W.
Thurm, Gail
Thurston, Jack
Tinkelman, Murray
Tommasino, David
Tora, Shinichiro
Townsend, Jr., Lloyd
Troop, Miriam
Trooper, David
Tsugami, Kyuzo
University of the Arts
Unruh, Jack
Usher, David P.
Valla, Victor
Vanacore, Fred
Vebell, Edward
Vero, Radu
Vetromile, Alfred G.
Vidal, Hahn
Vizbar, Milda Dravid
Waine, Stanley R.
Wald, Carol
Walker, Mort
Walling, Mrs. Dow
Walton, Thomas E.
Wapner, Raymond M.
Wasserman, Randi
Watts, Mark
Weber, Jessica M.
Weekely, Helen
Weiman, Jon
Weinberg, Harvey L.
Weisman, Jerome

Weiss, Morris S.
Weithas, Arthur
Wende, Phillip
Wenzel, David T.
Wergeles, Ed
Whelan, Michael R.
White, Mrs. Bernard
White, James D.
Whitmore, Mrs. Virginia
Whitney, Richard
Whyte, Andrew C.
Willbright, Frank
Willert, Beth Anne
Williamson, Mel
Willinger, Kurt
Wilson, George D.
Winkler, Roy
Winter, Donald M.
Winter, Thelma
Wise, Thomas M.
Witalis, Rupert
Witt, John
Wohlberg, Helen
Wohlberg, Meg
Wohlsen, Sr., Robert S.
Wolf, Ann
Wolfe, Jean E.
Wolfe, Tom
Wood, Rob
Wooten, Vernon E.
Yohe, Tom G.
Zaino, Carmile S.
Zander, Jack
Ziemienski, Dennis
Ziering, Bob
Zimmerman, Marie
Zinggeler, Jeff
Zuckerman, Paul

KIRCHOFF/WOHLBERG

866 United Nations Plaza, New York, NY 10017 212-644-2020
897 Boston Post Road, Madison, CT 06443 203-245-7308

ARTISTS' REPRESENTATIVE

ARTCO

Gail Thurm and Jeff Palmer

Serving New York City clients:
232 Madison Avenue, Suite 600, New York, New York 10016 (212) 889-8777

Serving clients outside New York City:
227 Godfrey Road, Weston, Connecticut 06883 (203) 222-8777

Additional work may be seen in American Showcase Vols. 10, 11 and 12.

Sally Vitsky

Al Pisano

Ed Acuna

Anne Cook

Bob Dacey

Dan Brown

Alain Chang

Gene Boyer

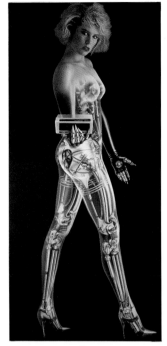

Beau and Alan Daniels

Rick McCollum

Lisa Henderling

George Angelini

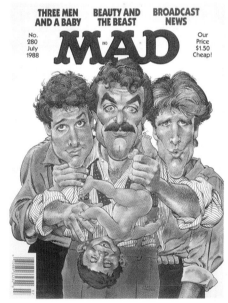

Mort Drucker

Kathy Jeffers

Jeff Cornell

OUR TEN COMMANDMENTS of ARTIST REPRESENTATION

1. We represent only artists we believe in and are totally committed to them.

2. We believe in being more than agents and become involved in the *total career* of the artists we represent.

3. We appreciate the problems of the artist and try, whenever possible, to alleviate these problems.

4. We also appreciate the problems of the art director: his client-agency relationship, tight deadlines and budget limitations and try to help him solve these problems whenever we can.

5. We believe in *full representation.* That means taking on only that number of artists that we can fully represent as well as insuring that each artist is non-competitive in style with other artists we represent.

6. We believe in giving *full service* to our artists and to the art director, promptly and professionally. Every client, no matter what the job price, deserves the very best we can offer.

7. We believe in being *flexible.* Business conditions change. The economy rises and falls. Accounts switch. We and our artists must adjust to all changes in order to successfully survive.

8. We believe in always meeting deadlines and always keeping a bargain. We and our artists are only as good as our word and our last job.

9. We believe in *BEING HONEST* at all times. With our artists. With the art director. With ourselves.

10. And finally, we believe in our *profession...* the profession of representing artists. We firmly believe that it is the most exciting and challenging profession anywhere and we are proud to be a part of it.

Barbara Gordon
Associates Ltd.
165 East 32 Street
New York, N.Y. 10016
212-686-3514

BOB BERRAN

JEFFREY MANGIAT

BOB JONES

GARRY COLBY

ELAINE GIGNILLIAT

ATTILA HEJJA

RAPIDOGRAPH®

Marv Espe creates drawings of many subjects with a wide range of fine-to-broad Rapidograph® line widths, stroked with deliberate spacing to show just the right white space in voids. In fact, the longer a viewer studies an Espe drawing, the more apparent it becomes that the voids be-

tween the lines are as carefully composed as the drawn lines, contributing to the imaging and modeling.

The drawings illustrated here are from what the artist calls "a visual documentary series," titled *Man's Hand in the Northland.* It is understandable if artist Espe's

talent is preoccupied with north country, since he received his formal art training in Chicago and Minneapolis, taught for five years in northern Minnesota, and was a design artist in a Minneapolis corporate graphic arts department.

He uses mixed media in some of his drawings, combining Rapidograph line art with colored gouache. Two such paintings have been added to the Koh-I-Noor Permanent Collection.

Dependability is what Marv Espe wants most from his drawing pens, the kind of dependability built into all Rapidograph pens, making them the most widely used technical pens among artists, design engineers, drafters, architects and hobbyists throughout the United States and Canada.

Develop your own skills and techniques with the Rapidograph pen. Tubular nib (in 13 line widths) can draw in any direction on virtually any drawing surface, includ-

These drawings by Marv Espe are copyrighted by the artist and may not be reproduced for any reason without written permission from the artist. (Approx size of original drawing images 15" x 13".)

ART
...from the North Country with Marv Espe

ing acetate and glass, with the ease of, and less pressure than a pencil grip.

"Get-acquainted" package is 3165-BX (choice of 5 line widths), offers a pen/ink combination savings. Single pens and studio sets available also. Ask your dealer or send the coupon for details. Koh-I-Noor Rapidograph, Inc., 100 North St., Bloomsbury, NJ 08804 (201) 479-4124. In Canada: 1815 Meyerside Drive, Mississauga, Ont. L5T 1G3 (416) 671-0696.

KOH-I-NOOR
RAPIDOGRAPH®
a rOtring company

NORMAN ADAMS

DON BRAUTIGAM

MICHAEL DEAS

MICHAEL DUDASH

MARK ENGLISH

ROBERT HEINDEL

STEVE KARCHIN

DICK KREPEL

SKIP LIEPKE

FRED OTNES

NORMAN WALKER

REPRESENTED BY: BILL ERLACHER ARTISTS ASSOCIATES
211 EAST 51 STREET, NEW YORK, N.Y. 10022
(212) 755-1365/6

ASSOCIATES: NICOLE EDELL

I llustration House is a unique gallery solely devoted to exhibiting and selling the original paintings and drawings of America's greatest illustrators who have taken their place as first-rank artists of universal appeal.

You'll be introduced to a wide selection of illustrative art, from its early masters to its contemporary notables, many of whom have been elected to the Society of Illustrators' Hall of Fame. Your hosts, Walt and Roger Reed, authors of "The Illustrator in America" and many other authoritative texts, are here to help you appreciate the pleasures of collecting, and to provide in-depth background information about this very special group of artists.

Illustration House publishes *The Illustration Collector*, a catalogue of selections from an inventory of paintings and drawings created for the publications that have made illustration history. Subscriptions, $12 for 3 issues or $3 for a sample copy.

Illustration House, Inc.
96 Spring St. • New York 10012 • (212) 966-9444

Providing collectors and museums with paintings and drawings of America's important Illustrators from the 1880's to the present.

Walt & Roger Reed, 7th floor, Tues.-Sat., 10:30 to 6

Franklin Booth (1874-1948), *May Dance*, pen & ink drawing, 14 x 10″.   Member: SI Hall of Fame

- Competitive cost
  - Flexibility in production time
    - Knowledge of sales reps
      - Service and fine quality
        - Financial stability

Can you expect all of these from your printer ?

The Society of Illustrators has come to us since its annual book, "Illustrators 23."

 DAI NIPPON is ready to serve you. You can get on the spot consultation from professional salesman.